YALE

SHAKESPEARE

SUPPLEMENTS

YALE SHAKESPEARE SUPPLEMENTS

A. M. Nagler, *Shakespeare's Stage*
Helge Kökeritz, *Shakespeare's Names*
Gerald Eades Bentley, *Shakespeare: A Biographical Handbook*

SHAKESPEARE

A Biographical Handbook

by GERALD EADES BENTLEY

New Haven, Yale University Press

Library of Congress catalog card number: 61–14997

Distributed in Great Britain, Europe, Asia, and
Africa by Yale University Press Ltd., London; in
Canada by McGill-Queen's University Press, Montreal; and
in Mexico by Centro Interamericano de
Libros Academicos, Mexico City.

Publication of this book has been aided by a
grant from the Kingsley Trust Association Fund
established by the Scroll and Key Society
of Yale College.

To
E. G. F. B.
with
admiration and gratitude

Preface

MY CHIEF CONCERN in this book has been to present the life of William Shakespeare and his methods of work with the strictest fidelity to the surviving documents, with the least personal bias I can achieve, and with a minimum of the cultural bias of our time toward the literary artist. Documents are stark, and to the untrained imagination they often seem dull. Nevertheless, I hope that by presenting the hundred or more surviving Shakespearean ones in the context of similar records, against the background of Elizabethan customs and prejudices, and in relation to one another, I can set up the essential outline of the man who lived in Stratford and London and not some fancied man our individual imaginations would like to create.

Such a summary book as this is dependent upon the painstaking efforts of hundreds of collectors and editors and scholars from John Ward in the mid-seventeenth century to Leslie Hotson in the mid-twentieth. In the course of three centuries they have unearthed the records upon which any truthful account of the life of William Shakespeare must be based. When I quote or summarize the documents they have found, I have generally, though not invariably, cited the name of the discoverer; but like everyone who writes about Shakespeare I am heavily indebted to their devoted and painful labors.

In the niggling and often exasperating chore of book-making I have had the conscientious and unstinted help of two successive research assistants, Remington Rose and James Redwine. I am grateful to them for their intelligent and cheerful assistance.

GERALD EADES BENTLEY

Princeton, N.J.
July 1961

Contents

CHAPTER 1

Shakespearean Biography in the Seventeenth Century and in the Twentieth

NO biography of Shakespeare was published during his lifetime, nor for ninety-three years after his death. This neglect of the greatest writer in the English language seems very strange, or even suspicious, to those modern readers and theater-goers who have some knowledge of the hundreds of biographies of lesser nineteenth- and twentieth-century men but comparatively little knowledge of the standards and customs of the seventeenth century. The question is often asked, Why didn't any of Shakespeare's friends or admirers write up his life?

The answer lies in the seventeenth-century standards of values. Every age, of course, has its own hierarchy of excellence, its own popular conventions as to what constitutes distinction, what human achievements are worthy of admiration and emulation, and the values of an earlier age frequently seem strange or distorted to later ones. In the mid-twentieth century, for example, the scientist stands high; few people now would question the judgment that Albert Einstein was a great man. But in Jacobean England the man of science enjoyed little admiration or respect, he was popularly feared or laughed at as a magician or an alchemist, his biography was seldom written. The men most popularly revered then were the religious figures and political leaders, and most of the biographies written were concerned with the lives of saints, bishops, and preachers, and, somewhat less frequently, the lives of kings, nobles, generals, and ministers of state.

Far down in the popular scale of values came the literary man, and the published biographies reflect this accepted estimate. Among several hundred English biographies written in the sixteenth and seventeenth centuries, there are only a few brief lives of poets of the time—George Herbert was one, and Francis Quarles, John Donne, and Sir Philip Sidney—and even in these few accounts the *literary* achievement of the man we know because of his poetry is often conspicuously neglected. For instance, Izaak Walton's famous life of John Donne first appeared in 1640 as a seventeen-page preface to an edition of eighty sermons preached by Doctor Donne, and in this short preface only one page and a little over are devoted to Donne's poetry. Walton revised and expanded his biography for later editions of the life in 1658, 1670, and 1675, the last of which is about twice as long as the original biography, but the new version adds only two or three pages on Donne the poet: the work was revised not to tell more about a great metaphysical poet but to paint a fuller and more effective portrait of the Reverend John Donne the saint. Izaak Walton wrote in conformity with the values of the mid-seventeenth century, not the mid-twentieth.

If readers of the time of Shakespeare and Donne thought the lives of contemporary poets of little significance, they thought the lives of playwrights to be of much less. To the serious-minded Englishmen who lived as subjects of Elizabeth I, James I, and Charles I, the theater was at best an institution to be tolerated for its entertainment values, at worst to be suppressed for its frivolity and immorality—as all theaters *were* suppressed by law as soon as the more sober-minded Englishmen got control of Parliament in 1642. The men who wrote for the theaters were, in the minds of most people, merely the less serious writers who worked for the players, and the acting profession, though an ancient one, was held in low esteem. During Shakespeare's lifetime, it is true, the actors of the London troupes became comparatively prosperous and consequently somewhat more respectable, but outside the metropolis many of the touring players were still classed as "rogues, vagabonds, and sturdy beggars," along with jugglers, palmists, fencers, bearwards, and unemployed sailors. The strait-laced continued to think of Shakespeare's London colleagues as belonging in this category.

When the social status of actors and their associates was so low, the writers who worked for the theaters were not likely to be accorded the recognition of biographies. Shakespeare is not alone in his obscurity: no single dramatist of his time found a contemporary biographer to collect and record the facts of his life for posterity. However popular the dramatists' plays were, their profession was one which then seemed too insignificant for their lives to be memorialized. No one wrote a life of Marlowe or Webster or Fletcher, or even of Ben Jonson, who was, among the learned and literary men who generally write the biographies, the most admired playwright of his age.

In the light of the hierarchy of values of the seventeenth century, then, it is not at all surprising that no life of Shakespeare or of any of the other dramatists who lived in London with him was written by a contemporary or a near-contemporary. In fact the first biography of Shakespeare was written nearly a century after his death, and it was merely incidental. Nicholas Rowe, who brought out an edition of the plays in 1709 —by which time all who had known the great dramatist were of course long since dead—combined a few stories he had heard, a few facts reported somewhat inaccurately from Stratford-upon-Avon, a number of pages of criticism of the plays, and some quotations from Dryden and Jonson to make for his edition an introduction of forty small pages, of which only about twelve are concerned with Shakespeare's life. Rowe's brief account was reprinted with minor variations a number of times in the eighteenth century, and his stories and facts constituted all the knowledge of Shakespeare the man that was generally available to eighteenth-century readers and writers. Later the romantic idealization of Shakespeare the poet and the enthusiasm for his poetry led in the nineteenth century to the addition of many dubious details to the popular biographies.

As a consequence of this early neglect and later credulity, many of the facts of Shakespeare's life have been irrecoverably lost, and many doubtful stories about him have become current. It will never be possible to write such a full and illuminating biography for the author of *Hamlet* and *King Lear* as have been written for Samuel Johnson or Charles Dickens or James Joyce. Letters to or from or about William Shakespeare have all disappeared except for a few referring to business transactions; diaries or accounts of his friends are gone. In the absence of personal material of this sort which provides the foundation of most biographies, the temp-

4

tation to amplify, to embroider, in fact to create an appealing and interesting figure, has been too strong for many of Shakespeare's admirers.

On the other hand, there are, surprisingly, still available to us many verifiable facts about the life of William Shakespeare from which we can, with care, put together a fairly clear picture of the greatest English writer. Such a biography, it is true, must be written almost entirely from the impersonal records left by Shakespeare's activities inside and outside the theater, records set down with no thought of recording the personality of an individual but intended merely to keep straight property transfers, or to preserve evidence of births, deaths, and marriages, or to keep account of public expenditures of money. Through the efforts of several generations of searchers, one hundred or more records of the activities of the dramatist have been unearthed since Rowe's short account of Shakespeare's life appeared in 1709—more records, in fact, than we have for any other playwright of the time except Ben Jonson. These documents must be the basis for any true picture of the man and his work.

The picture will be far from the complete and colorful one that most admirers of Shakespeare would like to have. It will not reveal his secret ambitions, his bitterest disappointments, or his subconscious desires; it will be a picture lacking in color and details. It will, however, show what the outlines of our conception of Shakespeare must be if the picture is to be related to the man who wrote the plays in the reigns of Queen Elizabeth and King James I and not to nineteenth- and twentieth-century stereotypes of what an ideal poet should be.

In the following chapters the documents that by chance survive from Shakespeare's career form the basic materials. They are set in the context of similar documents of the time so that their significance may be apparent, and their relation to one another and their cumulative implications are pointed out. Individual ideas of the sort of man Shakespeare was may differ, but, if they are to be worth serious consideration, they must fit into the outline made by the documents he left.

Legends

Legends always collect about the names of men who are widely discussed, whether they are hated or admired, and Shakespeare does not differ in this respect from Abraham Lincoln, or Julius Caesar, or Napoleon Bonaparte. Whenever there is a demand for stories, the stories appear, and it is common for the public memory to hold more tenaciously to the legend than to the fact. Writers to whom the documents from Shakespeare's life were not available and writers whose admiration of their own imaginings was greater than their respect for facts have made familiar a number of legends, or sometimes of fabrications, about Shakespeare that have gained currency by frequent repetition. Many of these popular legends began in the seventeenth century when most of the documents that establish the facts of Shakespeare's life were still unknown. Some of them may possibly reflect events in his life that did occur; others are either extremely dubious or entirely impossible in the light of what we now know; their currency simply shows that they set out events that many people would like to believe.

One of the earlier legends is found in the notes of John Aubrey, a feckless character of the late seventeenth century who collected masses of anecdotes, sayings, and facts about the lives of more than a hundred worthies of his own and the preceding age. He says that

M^r. William Shakespear. was borne at Stratford vpon Avon, in the County of Warwick; his father was a Butcher, & I have been told heretofore by some of the neighbours, that when he was a boy he exercised his father's Trade, but when he kill'd a Calfe, he would doe it in a *high style,* & make a Speech. There was at that time another Butcher's son in this Towne, that was held not at all inferior to him for a naturall witt, his acquaintance & co-etanean, but dyed young.

Since Aubrey wrote his note one hundred years or more after Shakespeare's boyhood, it is not likely that the Stratford neighbors—if Aubrey ever really talked to any of them—could have had any recollections of the boy William.

Similarly improbable is the story told about Shakespeare's early days in the theater, a legend which first appears about 130 years after the death of the actor—dramatist.

Shakespear, when he first came from the country to the play-house, was not admitted to act; but as it was then the custom for all the people of fashion to come on horseback to entertainments of all kinds, it was Shakespear's employment for a time, with several other poor boys belonging to the company, to hold the horses and take care of them during the representation;—by his dexterity and care he soon got a great deal of business in this way, and was personally known to most of the quality that frequented the house, insomuch that, being obliged, before he was taken into a higher and more honorable employment within doors, to train up boys to assist him, it became long afterwards a usual way among them to recommend themselves by saying that they were Shakespear's boys.

This story, like so many, bears the marks of its date of origin. When it first appeared, boy actors, who took all the women's roles in Shakespeare's time, had been gone from the London stage for a century. By that time no one was very familiar with the long and careful training required to make a good female impersonator out of a boy. If Shakespeare ever was attached to a London company as a boy (and such evidence as we have makes it seem unlikely that he came to London before he was a grown man), it is most improbable that he or any other carefully selected boy actor was ever excused from duties on or about the stage for any chores as unprofitable to the company as horse-tending.

In the early nineteenth century another appealing story about Shakespeare at the theater was circulated.

> It is well known that Queen Elizabeth was a great admirer of the immortal Shakspeare, and used frequently (as was the custom of persons of great rank in those days) to appear upon the stage before the audience, or to sit delighted behind the scenes, when the plays of our bard were performed. One evening, when Shakspeare himself was personating the part of a King, the audience knew of her Majesty being in the house. She crossed the stage when he was performing, and, on receiving the accustomed greeting from the audience, moved politely to the poet, but he did not notice it! When behind the scenes, she caught his eye, and moved again, but still he would not throw off his character, to notice her: this made her Majesty think of some means by which she might know, whether he would depart, or not, from the dignity of his character while on the stage.—Accordingly, as he was about to make his exit, she stepped before him, dropped her glove, and re-crossed the stage, which

Shakspeare noticing, took up, with these words, immediately after finishing his speech, and so aptly were they delivered, that they seemed to belong to it:

'And though now bent on this high embassy,
Yet *stoop* we to take up our *Cousin's* glove!'

He then walked off the stage, and presented the glove to the Queen, who was greatly pleased with his behaviour, and complimented him upon the propriety of it.

How pleasant to imagine the intimacy of the Queen and the poet! But unfortunately the facts do not at all support the anecdote. (1) There is no evidence whatsoever that Queen Elizabeth "was a great admirer of the immortal Shakspeare." (2) Though many plays were brought to court and acted before her there, Elizabeth never went to a public theater, nor did her successors James I and Charles I. It would have been a scandal of the time if she had gone, a scandal that would have been widely commented upon in the dispatches of ambassadors and in the letters of the numerous writers of political news who discussed the royal activities. (3) Plays in the Elizabethan theaters were never performed in the "evening," and (4) there was no scenery on the Elizabethan public stage for the Queen to sit behind. We do not need additionally to consider the story in the light of Elizabeth's nature and her concept of the august role of the crown to realize that this cozy story of the Virgin Queen and the Bard has all the marks of an uninformed romantic imagination of the nineteenth century.

A similarly romantic story was recorded at the very end of the seventeenth century in a few random remarks about Shakespeare made by Charles Gildon:

I have been told that he writ the scene of the Ghost in *Hamlet,* at his House which bordered on the Charnel-House and Church-Yard.

This story is eloquent of the popular urge to identify personal experience and literary creation. How thrilling to think of Shakespeare himself seeing ghosts in their appropriate habitat as he describes the reaction of Marcellus and Bernardo, on the battlements of Elsinore, watching the ghost of Hamlet's father walk

By their oppress'd and fear-surprised eyes,
Within his truncheon's length; whilst they, distill'd
Almost to jelly with the act of fear,
Stand dumb and speak not to him.

Thrilling, but highly unlikely. Shakespeare's plays, with the possible exception of the last two or three, were pretty surely not written in Stratford, the only place in which he ever lived in a house owned by himself or his family. The church at Stratford, like most Elizabethan churches, did have a charnel house for the disposal of human bones from old graves, but Shakespeare's father's house was more than a mile from the church and Shakespeare's own house, New Place, was about half a mile away.

But not all the legends about Shakespeare's composition of his plays are so improbable as this one about *Hamlet.* Early in the eighteenth century a better one appeared concerning *The Merry Wives of Windsor.* John Dennis rewrote this comedy in a form which he thought more acceptable to his time, and when in 1702 he published his version, which he called *The Comicall Gallant,* he wrote a dedicatory epistle in which he said of *The Merry Wives:*

That this Comedy was not despicable, I guess'd for several Reasons: First, I knew very well, that it had pleas'd one of the greatest Queens that ever was in the World . . . This Comedy was written at her Command, and by her direction, and she was so eager to see it Acted, that she commanded it to be finished in fourteen days; and was afterwards, as Tradition tells us, very well pleas'd at the Representation.

A few years later the story appears again, with another detail or two, in the life of Shakespeare that was prefixed to Rowe's edition of the plays:

Queen *Elizabeth* had several of his Plays Acted before her, and without doubt gave him many gracious Marks of her Favour: . . . She was so well pleas'd with that admirable Character of *Falstaff,* in the two Parts of *Henry* the Fourth, that she commanded him to continue it for one Play more, and to shew him in Love. This is said to be the Occasion of his Writing *The Merry Wives of* Windsor.

A year later Charles Gildon added a little more:

The *Fairys* in the fifth Act makes a Handsome Complement to the Queen, in her Palace of *Windsor,* who had oblig'd him to write a Play of *Sir John Falstaff* in Love, and which I am very well assured he perform'd in a Fortnight; a prodigious Thing, when all is so well contriv'd, and carry'd on without the least Confusion.

Though the truth of this story cannot be demonstrated now, it is much more in accord with known facts than the others. Shakespeare's company, the Lord Chamberlain's men, did indeed perform often before the Queen: there are still extant records of more than thirty performances by them at court, and though none of the records names the play performed, it is fairly certain that several of them were Shakespeare's, for he was the company's most active dramatist in this time, and the title pages of the first editions of two of his plays—including *The Merry Wives of Windsor*—say that they had been performed before the Queen. Hasty composition of *The Merry Wives of Windsor* is also likely enough, for all careful critics of the play have noticed that it contains an unusual number of minor contradictions and loose ends that could well be the result of haste. Furthermore the sequence of plays assumed in this legend—*Henry IV,* Part I, *Henry IV,* Part 2, and *The Merry Wives*—accords with such other evidence as we have, and most readers have noticed that the Falstaff of the comedy is not quite the same character as the Falstaff of the two history plays, a difference which could be accounted for by an arbitrary order that the shrewd fat man be shown in love. Finally, a royal commission to write the play would explain the somewhat irrelevant compliment to Queen Elizabeth which all critics have noticed in Act V, and if the performance had been planned for Windsor Castle, we might have the reason that *The Merry Wives,* unlike any other of Shakespeare's plays, is given a contemporary English setting.

Thus the story of Queen Elizabeth's order that Shakespeare prepare in two weeks a play about Falstaff in love coincides in a surprising number of details with known facts about the play and the dramatist. It cannot be definitely proved to be true, but most scholars would agree that it is one of the most probable of the many Shakespeare legends.

The conception, growth, and maturity of some of these legends can be observed as they pass from hand to hand. One of the most flourishing was first written down in the last quarter of the seventeenth century in the notes John Aubrey collected for the biography he wrote of Sir William Davenant, the poet laureate, dramatist, and theater manager who first introduced actresses on the regular London stage. Davenant, who had died only a few years before Aubrey wrote of him, had a wide reputation as a wit and a debauchee, and Aubrey's stories tend to conform to this general reputation. Aubrey says:

> Sr William Davenant Knight Poet Laureate was borne in ――――― street in the City of Oxford, at the Crowne Taverne. His father was John Davenant a Vintner there, a very grave and discreet Citizen: his mother was a very beautifull woman, & of a very good witt and of conversation extremely agreable. . . . Mr William Shakespeare was wont to goe into Warwickshire once a yeare, and did commonly in his journey lye at this house in Oxon: where he was exceedingly respected. I have heard parson Robert D [i.e. the Reverend Doctor Robert Davenant, brother of the poet laureate, a Wiltshire clergyman who outlived Sir William] say that Mr W. Shakespeare here gave him a hundred kisses. Now Sr. Wm would sometimes when he was pleasant over a glasse of wine with his most intimate friends e.g. Sam: Butler (author of Hudibras) &c. say, that it seemed to him that he writt with the very spirit that Shakespeare, and was seemed contentended [sic] enough to be thought his Son: he would tell them the story as above. in which way his mother had a very light report, whereby she was called a whore.

As Aubrey tells the story, it is an illustration of Davenant's admiration of the works of Shakespeare, of his conceit about his own writings, his loose tongue, and his elastic morals, all of which are compatible with other accounts of Sir William's life and character. But when Thomas Hearne retold the story in 1709 he altered the implications and added a few details.

> 'Twas reported by Tradition in Oxford that Shakespear as he us'd to pass from London to Stratford upon Avon, where he liv'd & now lies buried, always spent some time in ye Crown Tavern in Oxford, which was kept by one Davenant who had a handsome Wife, & lov'd witty Company, tho' himself a reserv'd and melancholly Man. He had born to him a Son who was afterwards Christen'd by ye Name of W^m. who prov'd a very Eminent Poët, and was knighted (by ye name of S^r. William Davenant) and ye said M^r. Shakespear was his God-father & gave him his name. (In all probability he got him.) 'Tis further said that one day going from school a grave Doctor in Divinity met him, and ask'd him, *Child whither art thou going in such hast?* to wch the child reply'd, *O Sir my God-father is come to Town, & I am going to ask his blessing.* To wch the D^r. said, *Hold Child, you must not take the name of God in vaine.*

About twenty years later Joseph Spence touched up the story at several points. His version says that "That notion of Sir William Davenant being more than a poetical child only of Shakspeare, was common in town," that the anonymous Doctor was "a head of one of the colleges, (who was pretty well acquainted with the affairs of the family)," and that the child mentioned Shakespeare by name, and he altered the reply of the head of the college to a more explicit statement, " 'Fie, child, (says the old gentleman), why are you so superfluous? have you not learned yet that you should not use the name of **God** in vain?' "

14

Finally the composition is given its most detailed and polished form in the notes of William Oldys in the middle of the eighteenth century:

> If tradition may be trusted, Shakespeare often baited at the Crown Inn or Tavern in Oxford, in his journey to and from London. The landlady was a woman of great beauty and sprightly wit, and her husband, Mr John Davenant (afterwards mayor of that city,) a grave melancholy man, who as well as his wife used much to delight in Shakespeare's pleasant company. Their son young Will Davenant (afterwards Sir William) was then a little school-boy in the town, of about seven or eight years old, and so fond also of Shakespeare, that whenever he heard of his arrival, he would fly from school to see him. One day an old townsman observing the boy running homeward almost out of breath, asked him whither he was posting in that heat and hurry. He answered, to see his *god*-father Shakespeare. There's a good boy, said the other, but have a care that you don't take *God's* name in vain. This story M^r [Alexander] Pope told me at the Earl of Oxford's table . . . and he quoted Mr Betterton the player for his authority.

These four consecutive versions of a late seventeenth-century story provide an excellent literary example of the way to develop an anecdote to gain point and carry conviction. They also demonstrate the growth and unreliability of a legend.

Many such stories about Shakespeare exist, and a few of them will be discussed later in relation to the recorded facts which they may possibly supplement. All of them display certain common characteristics of legends.

All the legends about Shakespeare, like the samples just quoted, begin with the recorded facts of the dramatist's life—his early years in Stratford, his long connection with the theater—and then they go on to supplement the facts with details in accord with the personal imaginative needs of the man who sets down the legend. But there is another large body of biographical writing about Shakespeare which gives much freer play to the irresponsible fancy. In this school the method of creating the writer's own image of the greatest English poet is a much more radical one: such a writer simply denies any recorded facts that do not fit his own picture of the author of the plays and substitutes others more to his taste. This method, practically unheard of among Shakespeare readers during the first two centuries after the poet's death, has had a strange vogue for more than a hundred years now, and many hundreds of books and articles which follow this popular method of recreating the past have been published.

One interesting thing about this spate of publications is that, though they are similar in the methods they use, they disagree violently in their conclusions. Some "prove" that Shakespeare's plays were written by Queen Elizabeth, some that they were written by Sir Walter Raleigh, many assert that the author was the Earl of Oxford, some that he was the Earl of Rutland, some the Earl of Derby; many declare that the author was Sir Francis Bacon who became Viscount St. Albans, some that he was the Earl of Salisbury, some the Earl of Southampton; one writer even believes that the plays were the work of Mary Queen of Scots. One of the most amusing arguments "proves" that Shakespeare's plays, plus a number of other plays of the time, were written by a nun named Anne Whateley. Other interesting candidates presented confidently at various times are an Italian named Michele Agnolo Florio, a Frenchman named Jacques Pierre, and an Irishman named Patrick O'Toole. Several writers assert that Shakespeare's plays and a number of others were written by Christopher Marlowe, who thus mysteriously lived on for about twenty years after his murder. Still other studies boldly create a person hitherto unknown; several of them propose that the writer of the plays was an illegitimate son of Queen Elizabeth, though this son is sometimes called Francis Bacon and sometimes William Shakespeare—but a different Shakespeare from the Stratford man—and one "proves" that he was the illegitimate son of the Earl of Hertford and Lady Catherine Grey who was raised by Shakespeare's mother and who wrote not only the works of William Shakespeare but those of Richard Barnfield, Christopher Marlowe, John Southerne, Thomas Morley, Thomas Campion, Henry Constable, John Dowland, and Alfonso Ferrabosco as well. Another fantasy is urged by several books and articles which "demonstrate" that the plays were written by a syndicate: one writer's stable is made up of Bishop Lancelot Andrewes, John Donne, Ben Jonson, Edmund Spenser, Sir Walter Raleigh, Sir Francis Drake, and others; another's is composed of the Earl of Derby, the Earl of Rutland, the Earl of Oxford, Christopher Marlowe, Sir Walter Raleigh, Viscount St. Albans, and the Countess of Pembroke; and a third writer accepts this latter syndicate, only substituting the Countess of Rutland for the untitled Marlowe. But perhaps the most interesting syndicate is the one proposed by Harold Johnson: the order of the Jesuits.

Violently as these writers disagree on the identity of the author of the plays, they all unite in believing that William Shakespeare the actor was not the man, and the great majority share the firm conviction that the author must have been a blue-blooded aristocrat. And they tend to be highly (and suggestively) emotional in their advocacy: they call the historic Shakespeare "the drunken illiterate clown of Stratford," "a lying rascal," "the Stratford poacher," "the drunken Warwickshire rustic," "the Stratford butcher boy," "the huckster Shagsper of Stratford."

Since the only common denominator in all these fervid rewritings of history is the indignant rejection of the actor from Stratford as the author of the plays attached to his name, they might all be lumped together as the anti-actor literature, or the anti-plebian literature, but the designation most commonly used is anti-Stratfordian.

It is significant that none of the enraged attacks on Shakespeare of Stratford nor any of the elaborate proposals of a substitute appeared in the seventeenth or the eighteenth centuries, or even in the early years of the nineteenth; in their full-blown form they are exclusively a post-Romantic Movement phenomenon. For the last hundred years the romantic image of what a great poet ought to be like has been astonishingly widespread among general readers not very well acquainted with the lives of most poets. This image has very little relation to most Renaissance poets, or to most modern poets, but it bears a striking resemblance to Percy Bysshe Shelley, the son of a baronet, and even more to the dashing and aristocratic George Gordon Byron, sixth Baron Byron. Obviously William Shakespeare of Stratford bore little resemblance in his background or in his career to either Shelley or Byron, and consequently literally hundreds of amateur literary critics in the nineteenth and twentieth centuries have been seeking to replace him as the author of the plays they all admire with someone more blue-blooded, or more mysterious, or both.

It is also noteworthy that the many people who have written to propose substitutes for the actor-dramatist themselves represent a variety of occupations, but among the journalists, accountants, lawyers, clergymen, chemists, doctors, politicians, and especially retired army officers, retired naval officers, and earnest ladies who advocate the dramatic accomplishments of the Earl of Rutland or the Earl of Oxford or Viscount St. Albans or Sir Anthony Shirley there have never been any professional scholars or critics of English literature. Anti-Stratfordianism has always been strictly an avocation for nonprofessionals.

Among this large body of amateur detectives a fascinating variety of methods and devices has been used. One man invented a large machine which picked out words from Shakespeare's works to form a long poem that revealed secrets of the author's life, such as the "fact" that the author, who was Bacon, composed *Hamlet* as a warning to his mother, Queen Elizabeth! Two others consulted a spiritualist medium named Hester Dowden, who put them in touch with the spirits of the Earl of Oxford, Viscount St. Albans, and William Shakespeare. Unfortunately the spirits told one man (a Baconian) that Viscount St. Albans had written most of the plays and, working through the same medium, told the other (Percy Allen, an Oxfordian) that the Earl of Oxford was chiefly responsible. Several investigators have sought permission to dig up graves in old churches and abbeys in search of sensational manuscripts which they had "positive proof" had been buried in the tombs; two or three have actually been given permission, but none has ever found any manuscripts. Elaborate ciphers and codes have been "discovered" by many of these earnest students and applied to the plays of the First Folio to reveal astonishing messages not only about the authorship of the plays but about all sorts of contemporary political and social events as well. It is odd how many people are impressed by alleged codes and ciphers, which are taken to be marvelous achievements of superintellects.

Though about thirty different men and women have been enthusiastically presented from time to time during the last hundred years as the author of Shakespeare's plays, two candidates have been more popular than the others. The first is Sir Francis Bacon, Baron Verulam and Viscount St. Albans, whose claims were first set forth at length in 1857 by Miss Delia Bacon in a book called *The Philosophy of the Plays of Shakspere Unfolded.* Miss Bacon really thought that the plays were written not by Francis Bacon alone but by a group inspired and directed by him; nevertheless she is generally, though somewhat inaccurately, thought of as the first great "Baconian." Her lead was followed by hundreds of fervid Baconians, like Ignatius Donnelly, a Minnesota politician who, in *The Great Cryptogram,* published in 1888, worked out complicated ciphers to reveal secret information, such as the unknown "fact" that in addition to Shakespeare's plays Bacon also wrote dozens of plays long attributed to other men, as well as Burton's *Anatomy of Melancholy* and the *Essays* of Montaigne. Other Baconians extended the claims of Bacon's authorship: John Elisha Roe, a Rochester lawyer, claimed that Bacon had also written works of Jonathan Swift, Addison and Steele, Daniel Defoe, John Milton, Thomas Hobbes, and Thomas Carlyle. It is difficult to believe that such fantasies have ever been taken seriously, but they have, and several Baconian societies, regular Baconian periodicals, and even a Baconian foundation have been set up by ardent believers —or perhaps ardent disbelievers is a better term.

For the last forty years, however, the appeal of the Baconians has been declining, except when stimulated by modern publicity methods, and Viscount St. Albans has been superseded among many anti-Stratfordians by the Earl of Oxford. The Delia Bacon of the Oxfordians is J. Thomas Looney, who in 1920 published *"Shakespeare" Identified in Edward de Vere the Seventeenth Earl of Oxford*. At present the Earl of Oxford societies and the Oxfordian publications and publicity releases are more in evidence than the Baconian ones. The impulses and the methods of the Oxfordians, however, are the same as those of the Baconians, except that they usually shy away from codes and ciphers. Other candidates continue to be argued for and written about, but none of them has as much publicity or as extensive organization as his supporters have given the Earl of Oxford.

Legends and fantasies have led to much popular confusion about the life of Shakespeare, a confusion that has not been reduced by the unfamiliarity of seventeenth-century standards of values or by the loss, in three and one-half centuries, of the personalia concerning a man now thought to be very great. Nevertheless many facts from Shakespeare's life are still available, and it will be the purpose of the following chapters to put those facts in such order and such context that a reasonably clear outline of the career of the author of the plays will appear.

CHAPTER 2

Shakespeare in Stratford-upon-Avon

THERE are many records of Shakespeare and his family in Stratford, where the poet was born, where he died, where his parents had lived before him, and where his children and grandchildren continued to live after his death. This Warwickshire market town near the center of England, now one of the chief tourist attractions of the British Isles, was, in the middle of the sixteenth century, a prospering small town, one of the three principal business communities of the county of Warwickshire. For the surrounding country it served as a market center where supplies could be purchased, and where farm produce was bought and sold: where grain was collected, cattle and sheep were marketed, wool and hides were processed and sold, cloth was woven and dyed, hides were tanned and made into gloves and shoes, rope and iron work were manufactured. It was not a large place as modern cities go, but the entire population of England then was around five millions, and Stratford was about as important in the nation as a town of 100,000 is in the United States today.

John Shakespeare, the poet's father, first appears in the town records in 1552. During the sixteenth century in the country about Stratford there were a number of different families with the name Shakespeare; it appears hundreds of times in court records, real estate transactions, local accounts, wills, and town minutes. Even in Stratford itself there was for a time another man, a shoemaker, with the same two names as Shakespeare's father.

The name was spelled in a variety of ways, for in the sixteenth and seventeenth centuries there were no generally accepted rules of spelling, and not only might a clerk be inconsistent in his spelling of a particular name but a man would spell his own name in different ways at different times. For instance, when Shakespeare bought a piece of property in the Blackfriars district of London, one of his associates in the purchase signed his name to the deed "Wm Johnsonn," and the very next day signed the mortgage for the same property "Wm Johnson." Most names, in fact, were spelled in a variety of ways. The great sea-captain to whom we often refer now as Sir Walter Raleigh spelled his own name in at least three different ways, Rawleyghe, Rawlygh, and Ralegh, and in referring to him his contemporaries spelled it seventy-three different ways, including Wrawly, Rolye, Reali, and Raleikk. The name of Shakespeare's fellow dramatist, Christopher Marlowe appears in various records of the family in Canterbury as Marlowe, Marloe, Marlo, Marlen, Marlyne, Merlin, Marley, Marlye, Morley, and Morle.

No one who has any acquaintance with sixteenth- and seventeenth-century records, therefore, is surprised to find that there are at least eighty-three different spellings of the name Shakespeare in extant records of members of the family, all the way from Shaksbye to Shagspere to Chacsper and even Shakeschafte. The now familiar spelling of Shakespeare (often written Shake-speare) is only the form most frequently used by the publishers of the early editions of the plays and the one usually adopted by modern publishers.

The poet's father had probably moved into Stratford from the village of Snitterfield, about five miles away. In Stratford he became a glove-maker and leather-dresser, as well as a dealer in farm produce. Before and for a few years after the poet's birth John Shakespeare must have been moderately prosperous, for he bought four different houses in the town at one time or another, and his name appears in various business and legal transactions. In these years he was also obviously well respected by his fellow citizens, for he was a member of the town council for twenty years, he held half-a-dozen different offices in the town government, and in 1568 he was elected mayor, in those days called bailiff in Stratford. When William was twelve or thirteen years old his father probably suffered financial reverses, for from that time until his death in 1601 records of law suits, property transactions, and actions of the town council indicate financial difficulties.

Shakespeare's mother was Mary Arden, from the village of Wilmcote, three or four miles from Stratford, where her father was a landowner who had once been the landlord of John Shakespeare's father. The couple had apparently been living in Stratford for a number of years before the poet was born. The baptisms of eight of their children and the burials of several of them are recorded in the parish registers at Holy Trinity Church in Stratford.

Such parish registers are a principal source of information about the lives of Englishmen in the sixteenth and seventeenth centuries. In the reign of Queen Elizabeth when baptism, marriage, and burial could normally be solemnized only in the church, every parish church in the kingdom was required by law to keep a record of these primal events, which consequently ought to be available in some parish register for every person living in England in the sixteenth and seventeenth centuries. Doubtless these records were once fairly complete, and in fact hundreds of thousands of them still exist, but in the last three or four hundred years many churches have burned with their records, many registers have been lost or stolen, and some have decayed beyond recovery. Even so, parish records of the baptism, marriage, or burial of important men may still be extant but undiscovered because no one knows in which of the thousands of parish registers to look.

The first record of the life of the dramatist William Shakespeare is found then, as one would expect, in the register of Holy Trinity Church, which served the parish of Stratford-upon-Avon. This large and handsome church, parts of which were built 300 years before Shakespeare was born, still stands, still serves as the parish church of the town of Stratford, and still displays the old parish register with its numerous entries about William Shakespeare and the members of his family. The first entry about William is found in the section headed "Baptismes" on the page for 1564, under the date April 26. In the Latinized form which the Stratford parish clerk at that time habitually used, the entry reads,

Gulielmus filius Johannes Shakspere

that is, William, son of John Shakspere.

This record shows only when the poet was baptized, not when he was born. Since the record on his tomb says that he died on the twenty-third of April, 1616, in his fifty-third year, his birthday must have been on, or not long before, the twenty-third of April. Actually the day of Shakespeare's birth is unknown, though the twenty-third is popularly accepted, on the assumption that when the infant was carried to the font he was three days old, a common age for baptism at the time. The date is a possible one and to many people has seemed highly appropriate because it is the day of St. George, patron saint of England. Unfortunately, appropriateness did not determine birthdays in the sixteenth century any more than in the twentieth.

In the next few years after 1564 there are records of the baptisms of five of Shakespeare's brothers and sisters in the registers at Holy Trinity, but neither there nor elsewhere is there a reliable record of the poet himself for eighteen years. Statements about his life in this period are all conjecture, but there are available facts about his family which make some guesses fairly plausible.

Two adjacent houses in Henley Street are now shown to all tourists in Stratford, the one as Shakespeare's birthplace and the other as his father's wool shop. It is possible that Shakespeare was born and grew up in one of these houses, for his father owned both of them and in time passed them on to the poet. One of them John Shakespeare bought in 1556, but it is not certain which one, it is not certain when he bought the other, and it is not certain that he ever lived with his family in either of them, though it is likely enough.

At the age of about six or seven Shakespeare probably started going to the Stratford grammar school, which is still standing about a quarter of a mile across town from his father's houses in Henley Street. The school had been endowed more than two centuries before Shakespeare was born, and in June 1553 when the town was given a charter by King Edward VI it became the King's New School of Stratford-upon-Avon. The sixteenth-century records of the Stratford boys who attended the school have long since disappeared, but

26

since it was the responsibility of the town officials and since Shakespeare's father was a member of the governing body, it is almost certain that he became a regular pupil at the King's New School.

During the year after the dramatist was born, his father was the town officer in charge of repairing the schoolmaster's house and later was active in selecting a new schoolmaster. The two men who were masters at the school between Shakespeare's seventh and fourteenth years were both well educated men—both of them had bachelor's and master's degrees from Oxford. They were paid better than most schoolmasters in England at the time, and the education they provided at the Stratford grammar school should have been better than the average.

In all the grammar schools of Elizabethan times, the training was almost entirely in Latin, the sixteenth-century language of international communication and international literature, and the first two or three years of a boy's attendance at these schools were devoted to a study, mostly by rote memorizing, of Latin grammar. The scene in *The Merry Wives of Windsor* (IV, 1) in which the Welsh schoolmaster Sir Hugh Evans puts his pupil William through his paces for the benefit of the boy's mother is a gently satiric picture of something very like what the young William Shakespeare must have experienced in his first few years at school. It may not be irrelevant that one of the Stratford schoolmasters of Shakespeare's time was Thomas Jenkins, a Welshman.

After their first years in Latin grammar the boys in Elizabethan grammar schools got Latin training in logic and rhetoric, in composition, in public speaking, in versification, and in the literature of a number of Roman writers. At the Stratford school, as in the others of the time, the boys would have read Terence, Cicero,

Virgil, Ovid, Horace, Juvenal, Martial, and Seneca. Shakespeare shows some familiarity with all these authors in his plays, and a special fondness for Ovid, whose poems he quotes with admiration and refers to again and again.

There is no certain evidence as to when or why Shakespeare left school. Nicholas Rowe in 1709 said firmly that

> His Father, who was a considerable Dealer in Wool, had so large a Family, ten Children in all, that tho' he was his eldest Son, he could give him no better Education than his own Employment. He had bred him, 'tis true, for some time at a Free-School, where 'tis probable he acquir'd that little *Latin* he was Master of: But the narrowness of his Circumstances, and the want of his assistance at Home, forc'd his Father to withdraw him from thence, and unhappily prevented his further Proficiency in that Language.

Rowe's information was derived from stories his friend Thomas Betterton, the great actor, had picked up at Stratford more than a century after the events in question, but the facts which have since been gleaned from town records contradict Betterton's stories in only minor instances. The municipal records at Stratford show that after a period of apparent prosperity John Shakespeare was in financial difficulties from 1577 until his death in 1601; that in 1587 he was superseded as an alderman; and that he seems to have lost much of his property before his death. It is not unlikely, then, that Shakespeare was indeed taken out of school to help in his father's business. There is no evidence of the date of such a withdrawal save for the fact that John Shakespeare's financial difficulties first become evident in the town records when the poet was about thirteen years old. One can guess that for several years thereafter Shakespeare worked for his father, or possibly was apprenticed to him.

After the baptismal record, the next solid piece of documentary evidence of what happened in Shakespeare's life—not problematical or conjectural—are the records concerning the marriage license issued in 1582 by the Bishop of Worcester, in whose diocese Stratford is located. Most marriages in Elizabethan times did not require a license; they were ordinarily performed by the parish priest in the parish church of either the bride or the groom. In Elizabethan society as in most modern societies the government was concerned to take precautions that no fraudulent or illegal marriages should take place: marriages in which one of the parties was already married, or in which one party was brought to the altar against his will, marriages in which the two parties were too closely related, or marriages of minors without the consent of parent or guardian. To prevent such irregularities the law required that the priest of the parish pronounce the banns for the wedding on three Sundays or holy days before the ceremony; that is, the priest must ask from the pulpit on three different occasions whether any member of the congregation knew of any legal impediment to the proposed union.

Sometimes the regular pronouncement of the banns on three Sundays or holy days would have required an inconvenient delay in perfectly legal weddings, especially when plans for the wedding matured just before periods of the year in which banns were prohibited, such as Advent and Lent. In 1582–83 the prohibited period covered by Advent ran from 2 December 1582 to 13 January 1583, and the prohibited period of Lent plus Easter week stretched from 27 January to 7 April

1583, so that in the four-month period from 2 December 1582 to 7 April 1583 there were only two weeks when the banns could have been read. The law took such situations into account, for it also provided that the bishop of the diocese could issue a license allowing the marriage to take place without banns, or with only one pronouncement of the banns. To make sure that there were no irregularities like those the banns were designed to prevent, the bishop required a written statement of the facts and reasons, and he further required two friends of the bride and groom or their families to post a bond indemnifying the bishop or his officials in case any later action or suit were brought against them for issuing the license. Though most couples were married with the usual banns, special licenses and bonds were not uncommon; the Bishop of Worcester issued 98 of them in the year Shakespeare's was granted.

Our next document is the bond, or obligation, for £40 which two friends, Fulke Sandells and John Richardson, signed when the Bishop issued a license to William Shakespeare and Anne Hathaway. This bond, with the crumbled remains of its seals, is still extant in the archives of the diocese of Worcester. Following the Latin statement of the principals, the sum, and the date (28 November 1582), comes the explanation in English:

> The condicion of this obligacion ys suche that if herafter there shall not appere any Lawfull Lett or impediment by reason of any precontract consanguinitie affinitie or by any other lawfull meanes whatsoeuer but that William Shagspere on thone partie, and Anne Hathwey of Stratford in the Dioces of Worcester maiden may lawfully solennize matrimony together and in the same afterwardes

remaine and continew like man and wiffe according vnto the lawes in that behalf prouided, and moreouer if there be not at this present time any action sute quarrell or demaund moved or depending before any iudge ecclesiasticall or temporall for and concerning any such lawfull lett or impediment, And moreouer if the said William Shagspere do not proceed to solennizacion of mariadg with the said Anne Hathwey without the consent of hir frindes, And also if the said William do vpon his owne porper costes and expenses defend & save harmles the right Reverend father in god Lord John bushop of Worcester and his offycers for Licencing them the said William and Anne to be maried togither with once asking of the bannes of matrimony betwene them and for all other causes which may ensue by reason or occasion thereof, That then the said obligacion to be voyd and of none effect or els to stand & abide in full force and vertue.

This bond showing that the Bishop of Worcester authorized the marriage after only one asking of the banns of William Shakespeare and Anne Hathaway is our only record of the event; the license itself and the allegation, or request for a license, have disappeared. (When the clerk entered a note of the license in the Bishop's register, he called the bride Anne Whateley of Temple Grafton, but this is pretty surely a mistake.) It is not known where the couple were married; they are not named in the records of marriages in the parish registers of Stratford, and the wedding probably took place in some nearby parish whose registers have now disappeared.

We know almost nothing about Shakespeare's wife. There were a number of Hathaways living in and about

Stratford, and it is not absolutely certain to which of these families Anne Hathaway belonged, but it is likely that she was one of the Hathaways who lived in the house now shown to tourists as Anne Hathaway's Cottage in the village of Shottery, about a mile from Stratford. At the time of the marriage license William Shakespeare was eighteen and his bride must have been twenty-six, since the inscription on her grave, beside that of her husband in the chancel of Holy Trinity Church, Stratford, says that she died on 6 August 1623 at the age of 67.

Just where or how this couple lived for the next few years is not known, but the records indicate that they always considered Stratford their home, even during the years when William Shakespeare was working in London. In Stratford their children and grandchildren were born and buried; in Stratford they were both themselves buried; in Stratford their surviving children were married and lived on; and in Stratford Shakespeare bought houses and lands, loaned and borrowed money, made investments, and finally made his will.

Shakespeare's three children were christened in Holy Trinity Church, Stratford, just as he and his brothers and sisters had been. The first child is found in the register of baptisms for the year 1583 under the date of May 26th:

Susanna daughter to William Shakespeare.

Twenty-four years later, in June 1607, this daughter was married in the same church to a rather distinguished Stratford physician named John Hall. They lived in Stratford, where their only daughter was baptized. This child, the dramatist's granddaughter, became Lady Bernard; at the time of her death in 1670 she was Shakespeare's last living descendant.

The second and third children of the poet were

twins; their christening is recorded in the book of baptisms of the parish register for the year 1584 (1585 in our calendar) under the date of February 2nd:

Hamnet & Judeth sonne and daughter
to William Shakspere.

Since these two names are somewhat unusual, one can make a fairly plausible guess that the godparents of the children were Hamnet Sadler, a baker of Stratford, and his wife Judith. They must have been good friends of the family, for Shakespeare left Hamnet Sadler a legacy in his will, of which Sadler was one of the witnesses.

Hamnet Shakespeare, the poet's only son, died at the age of eleven, and his burial is recorded in the parish register on 11 August 1596:

Hamnet filius William Shakspere.

His sister Judith lived to womanhood and married a Stratford man, Thomas Quiney. She had three sons all baptized in the parish church at Stratford: Shakespeare Quiney, Richard Quiney, and Thomas Quiney, who died at the ages of six months, twenty-one years, and nineteen years respectively, and who were all buried at Stratford. Judith herself died in 1662 and was also buried at Stratford.

Even this partial list of parish register entries shows how continuous was the association of Shakespeare and his family with the town of Stratford, and I have omitted about twenty-five of the register entries concerning his brothers and sisters, nieces and nephews. Though the dramatist himself must have been in London most of the time for more than twenty years, there is no evidence that he ever took his family out of Stratford, and when he accumulated capital he invested most of it in and about his home town.

When and why Shakespeare first left the town is unknown, though there is a seventeenth-century legend to explain his departure and more fanciful accounts from the nineteenth and twentieth. What we know for certain is that in 1592, ten years after his marriage, he had been in London long enough to have attracted some attention with his plays and to have aroused the jealousy of another dramatist.

The seventeenth-century legend concerning Shakespeare's departure from Stratford was first set down by a clergyman in a town not far from Stratford late in the seventeenth century or early in the eighteenth. Nicholas Rowe had also heard it, probably from the actor Thomas Betterton, and he told it as follows:

> He had, by a Misfortune common enough to young Fellows, fallen into ill Company; and amongst them, some that made a frequent practice of Deer-stealing, engag'd him with them more than once in robbing a Park that belong'd to Sir *Thomas Lucy* of *Cherlecot,* near *Stratford.* For this he was prosecuted by that Gentleman, as he thought, somewhat too severely; and in order to revenge that ill Usage, he made a Ballad upon him. And tho' this, probably the first Essay of his Poetry, be lost, yet it is said to have been so very bitter, that it redoubled the Prosecution against him to that degree, that he was oblig'd to leave his Business and Family in *Warwickshire,* for some time, and shelter himself in *London.*
>
> It is at this Time, and upon this Accident, that he is said to have made his first Acquaintance in the Play-house.

Whether this legend preserves the real reason for Shakespeare's departure from Stratford, no one knows; many do not like to believe it. Though Rowe's details

34

may be inaccurate, there are no sufficient grounds for denying the legend entirely, and Rowe was evidently not the only one who had heard it.

Neither this legend nor any known record makes it clear just when Shakespeare left Stratford or when he arrived in London. Presumably he was in Stratford in February 1585 when the twins, Hamnet and Judith, were baptized, but he had not necessarily remained there continuously in the five or six years before, and in 1592 when Robert Greene wrote about him he had evidently been in London for some time. The years of the late eighties are often called the Lost Years, for there are only conceivable identifications and faint rumors to show what Shakespeare might have been doing then. One of the more plausible of the identifications is the suggestion that he was the William Shakeshafte, probably an actor, who is mentioned in the will of Alexander Houghton, of Lea in Lancashire, a will executed on 3 August 1581. If so, he might have been a provincial player for several years before he got to London. Another rumor worth consideration because of its association with informed people is the one told to John Aubrey by William Beeston, an actor whose father was once an actor-associate of Shakespeare. Beeston said that

> He understood Latine pretty well: for he had been in his younger yeares a Schoolmaster in the Countrey.

But we have no proof of either play-acting or school-teaching in the provinces. Whenever and however he did get to London, it was there that his productive years, those to which all his literary achievement must be assigned, were spent. These years in London are best discussed separately in other chapters, but Shakespeare's connections with Stratford did not cease when he went to the capital; it is clear that the great London playwright never gave up his orientation to Stratford.

In Stratford Shakespeare made the first known investment of the money he began to accumulate in London; he bought a fine house for the establishment of his family in the town. This large stone house, called New Place, had been built about a century before by a member of the leading family of the town, Sir Hugh Clopton, who, like Shakespeare, had gone from Stratford to London; he had risen to be Lord Mayor there in 1491. New Place stood for more than 260 years. At the time Shakespeare bought it, the house was the second largest residence in Stratford. It was situated at the corner of Chapel Street and Chapel Lane, across from the Guild Chapel and from the Grammar School which he had probably attended twenty-five years before. The certified copy of the foot of fine, that is, the essential portion of the deed, was recorded 4 May 1597:

> Inter Willielmum Shakespeare querentem et Willielmum Underhill generosum deforciantem de vno mesuagio duobus horreis et duobus gardinis cum pertinenciis in Stratford super Avon . . . [Between William Shakespeare and William Underhill, gentleman, deforciant, concerning one dwelling house, two barns, two gardens and their appurtenances in Stratford-on-Avon . . .]

This large house remained in the hands of Shakespeare and his heirs for more than seventy years, until after the death of his last survivor, Lady Bernard. When Queen Henrietta Maria was traveling across England in July 1643 to join her husband, King Charles I, at Oxford, she spent two nights in Stratford as the guest of Lady Bernard at New Place. A house which was thought fit for the entertainment of the

Queen was a most unusual possession for a dramatist and actor to pass on to his children.

Within a year of his purchase of New Place, Shakespeare was storing grain in the barns on the property. The town records include an inventory of 4 February 1598 made to list the amount of grain being stored in the town and which shows:

> The noate of corne & malte Taken . . . Chapple Street Warde . . . Wᵐ Shackespere. x quarters. [80 bushels]

The fact that Shakespeare could buy and maintain such a house as New Place must have made his Stratford neighbors feel that he was one of the more notable of their townsmen in London. Some such estimate is indicated in the references to the dramatist in the correspondence of the Stratfordian Richard Quiney. The Quineys were themselves a rather prominent Stratford family: Richard's father had been bailiff (mayor) of the town three times, and Richard himself was bailiff twice; his son Thomas later married Shakespeare's daughter Judith. In January 1598 Richard Quiney was in London, apparently on business for himself, for his father, and for the town of Stratford. On 24 January 1598 his friend Abraham Sturley wrote him from Stratford saying that Richard's father had suggested that Richard get in touch with Shakespeare about buying some land near Shottery (where Shakespeare's wife had probably lived) and about helping to get the Stratford taxes reduced. Sturley writes in part:

> This is one speciall remembrance from vʳ fathers motion. It semeth bj him that our countriman, Mʳ Shaksper, is willinge to disburse some monei vpon some od yardeland or other att Shottri or neare about vs; he thinketh it a verj fitt patterne to move

him to deale in the matter of our tithes. Bj the in-
struccions v can geve him theareof, and bj the
frendes he can make therefore, we thinke it a faire
marke for him to shoote att, and not unpossible to
hitt. It obtained would advance him in deede, and
would do vs muche good.

Nine months later Richard Quiney was again in
London on business and while there addressed a letter
"To my Loveinge good ffrend & contreymann M^r
W^m. Shackespere deliver thees," asking Shakespeare as
a friend and fellow-Stratfordian to lend him £30 to
pay his London debts:

> Loveinge Contreyman, I am bolde of yowe as of
> a ffrende, craveinge yowre hclpe with xxx^li vppon
> Mr Bushells & my securytee or Mr Myttons with
> me . . . Yowe shall ffrende me muche in helpeinge
> me out of all the debettes I owe in London, I
> thancke god, & muche quiet my mynde which
> wolde nott be indebeted. I am nowe towardes the
> Cowrte in hope of answer for the dispatch of my
> Buysenes . . . My tyme biddes me hasten to an ende
> & soe I committ thys [to] yowre care & hope of
> yowre helpe . . . ffrom the Bell in Carter Lane the
> 25 October 1598. Yowres in all kyndenes Ryc.
> Quyney.

Whether Richard Quiney got the loan from his fellow townsman Shakespeare we do not know, but evidently his family in Stratford knew that he proposed to
try. About the same time that Richard wrote his request, his father Adrian Quiney, a mercer, or dealer in
textiles and fine fabrics, wrote to him from Stratford.
The elder Quiney mentions the request and asks his
son to buy knit stockings, apparently for the trade. His
letter is addressed "To my lovynge sonne Rycharde

Qwyney at the Belle in Carter Leyne deliver thesse in London" and begins:

> Yow shalle, God wylling, receve from your wyfe by ye baylye, thys brynger, aswrance of x^s . . . Yff yow bargen with Mr Sha. . or receve money ther- for, brynge your money home yf yow maye, I see howe knite stockynges be sold, ther ys gret byinge of them at Evysshome. Edward Wheat and Harrye, your brother man, were both at Evyshome thys daye senet [i.e. a week ago], and, as I harde, bestow 20^li. ther in knyt hosseyngs, wherefore I thynke yow maye doo good, yff you can have money.

On 4 November 1598 Abraham Sturley wrote again from Stratford. He too knew about the negotiations for a loan from Shakespeare. He addresses his letter "To his most lovinge brother, Mr Richard Quinej, att the Bell in Carterlane att London, geve these."

> V^r letter of the 25 of October came to mj handes the laste of the same att night per Grenwaj, which imported . . . that our countriman M^r Wm. Shak. would procure vs monej, which I will like of as I shall heare when, and wheare, and howe; and I praj let not go that occasion if it may sort to any indifferent condicions. . . . Abrah. Sturlej.

This correspondence of Stratford citizens about their townsman, or, as they say, "our countriman," William Shakespeare in London, reflects—as does the purchase of New Place—the rising standing of the Shakespeares in Stratford. As the fortunes of John Shakespeare declined, those of his son William rose, and it was probably at the instigation of the son, not the father, that the Shakespeares of Stratford were granted a coat of arms by the College of Heralds—in Elizabethan eyes the recognized external symbol of the standing of a gentleman.

In the archives of the College of Heralds in London are preserved several documents pertaining to the grant of arms for John Shakespeare: a rough draft of the original grant in 1596, a copy, a draft for another grant authorizing additions in 1599, and three drafts of the Heralds' defense in 1602 of twenty-three former grants, including the one to John Shakespeare. The first of these papers, now somewhat mutilated, shows the arms granted and the grounds for granting them.

> To all and singuler Noble and Gentilmen: of what Estate, degree, baring Arms to whom these presentes shall come. William Dethick Garter principall king of Arms sendethe greetinges. Knowe yee that whereas, by the authoritie and auncyent pryveleges perteyning to my office from the Queenes most excellent Maiestie and by her highnesse most noble & victorious progenitours, I am to take generall notice & record and to make declaration & testemonie for all causes of Arms and matters of Gentrie . . . Wherefore being solicited and by credible report [info]rmed, That John Shakespeare of Stratford vppon Avon, [in] the count[e of] Warwike, [whose] parentes [& late] grandfather for his faithful & va[leant service was advanced & rewar]ded [by the most prudent] prince King Henry the seventh of [famous memorie, sithence which tyme they have] continewed in those partes being of good reputacon [& credit, and that the s]aid John hath maryed the daughter [& one of the heyres of Robert Arden of Wilmcoote in the said] Counte esquire, and for the encouragement of his posterite to whom [these achivmentes by the a]uncyent custome of the Lawes of Arms

maye descend. I the Said G[arter king] of Arms
have assigned, graunted, and by these presentes
confirmed: This sh[ield] or [cote of] Arms, viz.
Gould, on a Bend Sables, a Speare of the first
steeled argent. And for his creast or cognizaunce
a falcon his winges displayed Argent standing on
a wrethe of his coullers: suppo[rting] a Speare
Gould steeled as aforesaid sett vppon a helmett
with mantelles & tasselles as hath ben accustomed
and doth more playnely appears depicted on this
margent: Signefieinge hereby & by the authorite of
my office aforesaid ratefieing that it shalbe lawfull
for the said John Shakespeare gentilman and for
his children yssue & posterite (at all tymes & places
convenient) to beare and make demonstracon of
the same Blazon or Atchevment vppon theyre
Shieldes, Targetes, escucheons, Cotes of Arms, pen-
nons, Guydons, Seales, Ringees, edefices, Buyld-
inges, vtensiles, Lyveries, Tombes, or monumentes
or otherwise for all lawfull warlyke factes or ciuile
vse or exercises, according to the Lawes of Arms,
and customes that to gentillmen belongethe without let or interruption of any other person or persons for vse or bearing the same. In witnesse & per-
petuall remembrance hereof I have herevnto sub-
scribed my name & fastened the Seale of my office
endorzed with the signett of my Arms. At the office
of Arms London the xx daye of October . . . 1596.

The coat of arms sketched in the margin by William
Dethick, who was the principal officer in charge of heraldic matters in the capital, may be seen carved on the
monument above William Shakespeare's grave and on
the tombstone of his daughter Susanna; it is often
stamped on the bindings of editions of Shakespeare's
plays. After the grant of arms and the purchase of New

41

Place, Shakespeare usually appears in legal records of property transactions, especially those about Stratford, as "William Shakespeare of Stratford upon Avon, gentleman"; in the parish-register entry of his burial he is called "Will. Shakspere, gent."

The money that he was making in London Shakespeare continued to invest in and about Stratford. In 1602 he bought from William and John Combe 107 acres of farm land north of town, for which he agreed to pay £320. The deed of conveyance for this piece of property is now in the Birthplace Museum at Stratford.

This Indenture made the firste daie of Maye, in the fowre and fortieth yeare of the raigne of our Soueraigne Ladie Elizabeth [1602] . . . Betweene William Combe of Warrwicke, in the countie of Warrwick, Esquier, and John Combe of Olde Stretford, in the countie aforesaide, gentleman, on the one partie, And William Shakespere of Stretford vppon Avon, in the countie aforesaide, gentleman, on thother partye, Witnesseth that the saide William Combe and John Combe, for and in consideracion of the somme of three hundred and twentie poundes of currant Englishe money to them in hande at and before the ensealinge and deliuerie of theis presentes well and trulie satisfied, contented and paide . . . by theis presentes doe fullye, clearlie and absolutelie alien, bargayne, sell, give, graunte and confirme vnto the saide William Shakespere, All and singuler those errable landes, with thappurtenaunces . . . conteyninge by estimacion one hundred and seaven acres, be they more or lesse . . . In wytnes wherof the parties to theis presentes have enterchangeably sette their handes and seales, the daie and yeare first aboue written, 1602. W. Combe. Jo. Combe . . . Sealed and de-

> liuered to Gilbert Shakespere to the vse of the
> within named William Shakespere, in the presence
> of Anthony Nasshe, William Sheldon, Humfrey
> Maynwaringe, Rychard Mason, Jhon Nashe.

Gilbert Shakespeare, to whom the deed was delivered, was the poet's younger brother; evidently Shakespeare was not in Stratford at the time, and one would guess that he was in London at the Globe.

Shakespeare's affairs were evidently going very well indeed, for in the same month in which he purchased the farm land, he bought a cottage across Chapel Lane from the garden of New Place; the document recording the transaction is also preserved in the Birthplace Museum. Surveys of 1604 and 1606, now in the Public Record Office in London, record this property as belonging to Shakespeare, and in his will he asked his daughter Judith to surrender her interest in it to her sister Susanna Hall. Evidently she did, for another survey of 1617 records the payment of two shillings and six pence by

> John Haule gen. and Susan his wief for the Fyne
> of admyttance of the said Susan unto one cottage
> in Stratford after the decease of Wm. Shakespere,
> gen. late father of the said Susan.

In 1605 Shakespeare made the largest investment which is known to us: he bought an interest in the lease of Stratford tithes. Such an investment was a rather common one in the time, but it derives from a complicated historical situation arising out of the dissolution of the monasteries a generation before Shakespeare was born.

When the monastic establishments were abolished in the reign of Henry VIII, their vast land holdings, for which the tenants paid rents or tithes, had to be legally transferred to other owners. In 1553, when the town of Stratford received its charter of incorporation, a good part of the tithes from land which had been controlled by the old monastic establishment in Stratford was made over by the King to the town corporation. These rentals were the Stratford tithes; they were not voluntary donations from pious people to a church. The Corporation of Stratford made long-term leases of these tithes to various individuals, who collected them and paid an annual fee to the town, or else in turn made subleases to others. It was one of these subleases that Shakespeare bought from a man named Ralph Huband. He agreed to pay £5 a year to a creditor of Huband's named John Barker and £17 a year to the Stratford Corporation, and to collect the tithes himself or through an agent. The very long deed of assignment of the tithe lease from Ralph Huband to William Shakespeare is now in the Birthplace Museum. It begins and ends as follows:

> This Indenture made the ffowre & twentythe daye of Iulye in the yeares of the raigne of our Soueraigne Lord Iames by the grace of god of England . . . the Thirde . . . Betweene raphe Hubande of Ippesley in the countye of Warr. Esquier, on thone parte, and William Shakespear of Stratforde vpon Avon in the sayed countye of Warr., gent., on thother parte . . .
> In witnes whereof the partyes abovesayed to thees presentes interchangeablie have sett their seales the Daie & yeare ffyrst above written. Raffe Huband . . . Sealed and delivered in the presence of William Huband Anthony Nasshe Fra: Collyns.

Francis Collins was the lawyer who, eleven years later, drew up Shakespeare's will.

Six years after his purchase of an interest in the tithes, Shakespeare was involved in legal action designed to clarify and define the respective responsibilities of the various individuals who had leased Stratford tithes. Since this action arises directly out of the lease just discussed, we will consider it here, skipping for the moment Shakespeare's activities in Stratford between 1605 and 1611.

There are two documents of 1611 in the Stratford archives which are concerned with a complaint brought in the Court of Chancery by three of the lease-holders of the tithes asking the court to make a formal decision about the amount of rent to be paid by each lease-holder. They complain that some of the leases are specific about the rent to be paid by each individual and that other leases are not, and that the uncertainty jeopardizes the interests of those whose rents are specified. The first document, the complaint, outlines an action brought by

> Richard Lane of Awston in the county of Warwicke, esquire, Thomas Greene, of Stratford uppon Avon in the said county of Warwicke, esquire, and William Shackspeare, of Stratford uppon Avon aforesaid in the said countye of Warwicke, gentleman.

Concerning Shakespeare's holdings, the complaint says:

> Your oratour William Shackspeare hath an estate and interest of and in the moyty or one half of all tythes of corne and grayne aryseing within the townes villages and fieldes of Old Stratford, Byshopton and Welcombe, being of and in the said parishe of Stratford, and of and in the moity or half of all tythes of wooll and lambe, and of all

45

small and pryvy tythes, oblaciones, and alterages arisynge or increasyng in or within the wholl parishe of Stratford-upon-Avon aforesayd, for and duringe all the residue of the said terme, being of the yearely value of threescore powndes.

And the complaint later notes the present inequity by which Shakespeare and Lane are often forced to pay extra rent in order to avoid default because the other leases have been vaguely or inaccurately drawn:

. . . your oratours Richard Lane and William Shackspeare, and some fewe others of the said parties, are wholly, and against all equity and good conscience, usually dryven to pay the same for preservacion of their estates.

The other document at Stratford concerned with this inequity is a draft of the answer of one of the tithe holders, William Combe. He agrees to pay more rent.

In 1607, two years after the purchase of the Stratford tithes, the record of the marriage of Shakespeare's elder daughter Susanna appears in the Stratford marriage registers:

Junij 5   John Hall gentleman & Susanna Shaxspere.

John Hall became quite well known as a physician, but the records of his life before his marriage are obscure because of the commonness of his name. Since he was thirty-two years old at the time of his marriage, he could have been the John Hall of Worcestershire who was at Balliol College, Oxford, and received degrees of B.A. in 1595 and M.A. in 1598. In Stratford the Shakespeare connection was cherished by the Halls. Both Susanna and her husband were buried in the row of five Shakespeare graves inside the chancel of Trinity Church; on Dr. Hall's grave the arms of Shakespeare are impaled with those of Hall, and the inscription on his gravestone reads:

HEERE LYETH Y^E BODY OF IOHN HALL

GENT. HEE MARR[IED] SVSANNA, Y^E DAUGHTER

& COHEIRE, OF WILL: SHAKESPEARE, GENT. HEE

DECEASED NOVE[MBER] 25 A[NNO] 1635, AGED 60.

Susanna's grave in the same Shakespeare row and beside that of her husband records her death on 2 July 1649 and further emphasizes the Shakespeare connection. The verse on the stone begins,

Witty above her sexe, but that's not all,
Wise to salvation was good Mistris Hall,
Something of Shakespeare was in that, but this
Wholy of him with whom she's now in blisse

For a time after their marriage, Shakespeare's daughter and her husband lived in a handsome house on the street called Old Town; the building, Hall's Croft, is still standing. After Shakespeare's death the Halls lived in New Place.

Before and after his daughter's marriage, in 1604, 1608, and 1609, Shakespeare was involved, through an attorney, in actions in the Stratford Court of Record for the collection of debts owed him by Philip Rogers and John Addenbrooke of Stratford. The debts were small, as was usual in this court, and little is known about the defendants or the circumstances which lay behind the actions. The records serve, however, as further evidence of Shakespeare's continued involvement in Stratford during the years when his principal activities were in London.

In 1610 there was another land transaction between Shakespeare and his friends William and John Combe,

from whom he had acquired his farm land; it is recorded in the *Pedes Finium Warwick,* now preserved in the
Public Record Office at London:

> Inter Willielmum Shakespere generosum queren-
> tem et Willielmum Combe armigerum et Johan-
> nem Combe generosum deforciantes de centum et
> septem acris terre et viginti acris pasture cum per-
> tinenciis in Old Stratford et [Stratford] super Avon
> ... [Between William Shakespere gentleman plain-
> tiff and William Combe esquire and John Combe
> gentleman defendants, concerning one hundred
> and seven acres of land and twenty acres of pasture
> with their appurtenances in Old Stratford and
> Stratford-upon-Avon]

There is some uncertainty whether this document
records an additional purchase of twenty acres of pasture land to be added to the 107 acres of land which
Shakespeare had bought from William and John
Combe in 1602, or whether the 20 acres of pasture were
really a part of the original purchase and this document is merely a confirmation and further recording
of the original transaction. In either case Shakespeare's
friendly relationships with the Combes and his continued interest in securing or extending his Stratford
estate are made evident.

The John Combe of this sale was a well-to-do Stratfordian, nephew of the William Combe associated with
him and a member of a numerous family of Combes in
Warwickshire. Like Shakespeare, John Combe, with
Thomas Greene, John Sadler, Julius Shaw, and other
prosperous citizens of Stratford, made contributions in
1611 to a fund for prosecuting a bill about the improvement of the highways, then before Parliament. The list
of contributors, now preserved in the Birthplace Museum at Stratford, contains 72 names. It is headed:

Wednesdaye the xjth of September 1611
Colected towardes the charge of prosecutyng the
Bill in parliament for the better Repayre of the
highe waies and amendinge diuers defectes in the
Statutes alredy made.

One of the names is

Mr William Shackspere

John Combe was evidently not only an associate but
also a friend of the dramatist, for when he made his will
on 28 January 1613 disposing of a large amount of
property, Shakespeare was one of several Stratford
friends to whom he left legacies.

In the name of God, amen! I John Combe, of Old
Stretford in the county of Warwick, gent., being
both in perfect health and memory, God be
thanked, do make, ordain, and declare my last
will and testament in manner and form following,
that is to say, first I commend my soul to God my
Maker, hoping and stedfastly believing that
through the only merits of Jesus Christ, my alone
Saviour and Redeemer, I shall after this life ended
be partaker of the life everlasting, and my body to
be buried in the Parish Church of Stretford upon
Avon in the said county of Warwick . . . Item, I
give . . . To Mr. William Shackspere five pounds.

After John Combe's death in July 1614 and following
the instructions in his will, a monument was erected
over his grave in the chancel of Trinity Church and
near the spot where Shakespeare was to be interred
about two years later. It is in the light of these facts
that we must view the epitaph which popular legend
says Shakespeare wrote on his well-to-do friend. In a

collection of epitaphs published in 1618 by Richard Brathwaite in a volume called *Remains after Death* appeared this one:

> An Epitaph vpon one Iohn Combe of Stratford vpon Auen, a notable Vsurer, fastened vpon a Tombe that he had caused to be built in his life time.

> Ten in the hundred must lie in his graue,
> But a hundred to ten whether God will him haue?
> Who then must be interr'd in this Tombe?
> Oh (quoth the Diuell) my *John a Combe.*

Brathwaite mentioned no author for the epitaph, and the essential idea in the couplets—i.e. ten in the hundred; a hundred to ten—had appeared in earlier versions of epitaphs which named neither any particular usurer (which is implied in the 10 per cent interest) nor any author. Between 1618, when Brathwaite published the verses, and 1709, when Nicholas Rowe wrote his brief life of Shakespeare, the epitaph was copied with minor variations by a number of writers, several of whom attributed it to William Shakespeare.

The most familiar version of the attribution is one which was written by Nicholas Rowe, who says that in Shakespeare's years of retirement at Stratford John Combe was a particular friend and that

> in a pleasant Conversation amongst their common Friends, Mr. *Combe* told *Shakespear* in a laughing manner, that he fancy'd, he intended to write his Epitaph, if he happen'd to out-live him; and since he could not know what might be said of him when he was dead, he desir'd it might be done immediately: upon which *Shakespear* gave him these four Verses.

Rowe then quotes the epitaph and concludes:

> But the Sharpness of the Satyr is said to have stung
> the Man so severely, that he never forgave it.

No one knows how much truth, if any, there is in
this story. Certainly the essential part of the epitaph
without any reference to Combe was known and recorded before Shakespeare retired to Stratford; certainly it is not true that the lines caused any great
estrangement, for John Combe left Shakespeare a legacy, and the dramatist in his own will left his sword to
John Combe's nephew Thomas. It is possible, however,
that Shakespeare in some convivial meeting did *adapt*
the popular lines to his friend John Combe.

In the last two years of his life Shakespeare, with a
number of other Stratford citizens, was peripherally
involved in a very complicated and impassioned real
estate controversy generally known as the Welcombe
Enclosure. Welcombe was a village and farming area
about one mile north of the town of Stratford. Here
Shakespeare owned tithe rights, and here a number
of other Stratford citizens, as well as the corporation of
the town, had interests. Late in 1614 some major land-
owners in the Welcombe area—Arthur Mainwaring,
William Replingham, and William Combe, nephew of
Shakespeare's friend John Combe and brother of
Thomas Combe to whom Shakespeare was to leave his
sword—proposed to enclose the land.

Land enclosure aroused violent emotions in the sixteenth and seventeenth centuries. Essentially it was an
agricultural reorganization which replaced medieval
methods of land tenure and cultivation with more modern ones, and like all such changes that bring about
economic gain for some and losses for others it aroused
most violent passions. According to the old system, the
renters of agricultural land leased several long narrow

strips of unfenced ground, not adjacent to one another, and they all grazed their stock together on "common" land which was not fit for cultivation or which was lying fallow. Such an ancient scheme was intended to be fair to all, but it was in fact extremely wasteful, since the best farmers were forced to handle their land and their stock pretty much the same as the worst farmers handled theirs. Enclosure simply abolished the old system of farming in narrow strips and grazing in common, and substituted fenced fields and pastures more or less as we know them now, and this is what Mainwaring, Replingham, and William Combe proposed to do with their land in Welcombe near Stratford. Some men saw the advantage, but many more were opposed, and in 1615 several people were assaulted over the digging of a boundary ditch by William Combe's men, and the women and children of Stratford came out and filled in the ditch.

The Corporation of Stratford was much concerned with the proposal to enclose and with the various legal steps to accomplish it, because they feared that their tithes or rentals would fall off if some of the farming strips became pasture land, and that some of the poor people of Stratford would be further impoverished. The town clerk, Thomas Greene, was very active in following the different steps in the controversy and in reporting the actions and sentiments of people concerned, including William Shakespeare, whom he called his cousin, though no one understands just how they were related. Shakespeare's own concern with the highly emotional and misguided controversy over the proposed Welcombe enclosure was only slight and comes about because of the part of the Stratford tithes in Welcombe which he owned. Numerous documents about this controversy still exist in Stratford and in London, and a great many people were more involved with it than was Shakespeare. His part appears prominent only when documents concerning him are extracted from the large mass of papers, as we select them here.

The first Shakespeare document in the mass of Welcombe enclosure papers is an entry made by Thomas Greene in a survey of the land-holders in the controversial area:

> 5 Septembris. 1614.
> Auncient ffreeholders in the ffields of Oldstratford and Welcombe.
> Mr Shakspeare. 4. yard Land. noe common nor ground beyond gospell bushe, noe grownd in Sandfield, nor none in slowe hill field beyond Bishopton nor none in the enclosure beyond Bishopton.

The second document in the series is an agreement —made 28 October 1614 by William Replingham, one of the men proposing to enclose his land—that Shakespeare and Thomas Greene will not suffer loss from their tithes because of his enclosure, or that if they do he will recompense them. The original is not extant, but a contemporary copy is preserved in the Birthplace Museum at Stratford.

> Vicesimo octavo die Octobris, anno Domini 1614. Articles of agreement indented made betweene William Shackespeare, of Stretford in the county of Warwicke, gent., on the one partye, and William Replingham, of Greete Harborowe in the countie of Warwicke, gent., on the other partie . . . the said William Replingham, for him, his heires, executours and assignes, doth covenaunte and agree to and with the said William Shackespeare, his heirs and assignes, That . . . William

53

Replingham . . . shall, uppon reasonable request, satisfie, content and make recompence unto him, the said William Shackespeare or his assignes, for all such losse . . . as he . . . and one Thomas Greene, gent., shall . . . sustayne or incurre for or in respecte of the increasing [error for *decreasing*] of the yearelie value of the tythes they the said William Shackespeare and Thomas doe joyntlie or seuerallie hold and enioy in the said fieldes, or anie of them, by reason of anie inclosure or decaye of tyllage there ment and intended by the said William Replingham.

Thomas Greene at this time was apparently not averse to the proposed enclosure and merely joined with Shakespeare in getting a precautionary guarantee from William Replingham that they should not sustain any loss. The Stratford corporation, however, was very fearful of the prospect, and Thomas Greene, as town clerk, later appears keeping track of negotiations and sounding out people for the corporation. A few remaining pages from Greene's business memoranda or diary, now preserved in the Birthplace Museum, display these activities, which now and then involve Shakespeare. In November 1614 Greene was in London, and when Shakespeare came to the city with his son-in-law John Hall, Greene went to see them and noted Shakespeare's report of the intentions of the enclosure proposers.

Jovis 17 No. At my Cosen Shakspeare commyng yesterday to towne I went to see him howe he did he told me that they assured him they ment to inclose noe further then to gospell bushe & so vpp straight (leavyng out part of the dyngles to the ffield) to the gáte in Clopton hedge & take in Salisburyes peece: and that they meane in Aprill to

servey the Land & then to gyve satisfaccion & not
before & he & Mʳ Hall say they think there will
be nothyng done at all.

In December, when Thomas Greene was back in
Stratford, he noted that when Mr. Replingham was in
town he had tried to see the gentleman at the Bear
Tavern and at Shakespeare's house, New Place.

10 Dec. that the survey there was past, & I came
from Wilson to look Mʳ Replingham at the beare
& at new place but myssed him & on the narowe
sid but he was not to be spoken with.

Two weeks later there was a meeting of the Stratford
corporation ("A Hall") which sent out reports and letters about the enclosure, and Greene records,

23 Dec. 1614. A Hall. L[ett]res wrytten one to Mʳ
Manneryng another to Mʳ Shakspeare with almost
all the com[panyes] hands to eyther: I alsoe wrytte
of myself to my Cosen Shakespeare the Coppyes of
all our oathes m[a]de then alsoe a not of the In-
convenyences wold gr[ow] by the Inclosure.

On 9 January Greene inserted a reminder to himself
that he and Shakespeare had an agreement with William Replingham about their rights made three
months before:

r[emember] . . . 9 Jan. 1614 [i.e. 1615 modern cal-
endar] Mʳ Replyngham 28 Octobris articled w[i]th
Mʳ Shakspeare & then I was putt in by T. Lucas.
. . .

Two days later Greene added another note:

On Wednesday, being the xjᵗʰ day . . . At night Mʳ
Replingham supped w[i]th me and Mʳ Barnes was
to beare him Company, where he assured me be-

fore Mr Barnes that I should be well dealt w[i]th-
all, confessyng former promises by himself M^r
Manneryng & his agreement for me w[i]th my
cosen Shakpeare. . . .

Finally the last of Thomas Greene's memoranda concerning Shakespeare is a reminder of a remark made
by the dramatist:

Sept. W Shakspeares tellyng J Greene that J was
not able to beare the encloseinge of Welcombe.

In the great mass of papers about the proposed enclosure at Welcombe, Shakespeare's name appears only
a few times, and it is clear that he was not very active
in the controversy. What one does see in the quoted
documents is Thomas Greene's acceptance of Shakespeare as one of the prominent citizens of Stratford,
and also further evidence of the poet's care about the
investments he had made to establish and provide for
his family in Stratford.

About six weeks before Shakespeare's death the marriage of his second daughter, Judith, to Thomas
Quiney is recorded in the Stratford parish registers:

Feabruary 10 Tho Queeny tow Judith Shakespeare.

The Quineys had been a Stratford family for several
generations. Thomas was the son of Richard Quiney,
the Stratford mercer whose correspondence several
times mentions Shakespeare (see above, pp. 37–39); he
was himself a vintner and kept the tavern called The
Cage, on the corner of High Street and Bridge Street in
Stratford.

For reasons unknown, Thomas Quiney and Judith
Shakespeare were married at the Stratford church during Lent, when weddings were supposed to take place
only with the Bishop's special license. Why the couple

did not secure such a license no one knows, but they were married in the church nevertheless, and for this offense they were excommunicated by the Bishop of Worcester a few months later.

Two weeks before Judith's marriage Shakespeare had drawn up his will, and two months after this original draft was made he revised it to take account of her married state. This will is now preserved at Somerset House in London, where most of the extant wills of the time, like that of Shakespeare's friend John Combe, are filed. In general form and character it is like hundreds of other extant wills made by Englishmen in the reign of James I. The document was drawn up by Francis Collins, the lawyer who had handled Shakespeare's real estate affairs and who shortly afterward became Steward to the Corporation of Stratford. Since he was made one of the two overseers of the will, Shakespeare must have had confidence in him.

In its main provisions the will runs as follows:

Vicesimo Quinto die Martij . . . Annoque
domini 1616

In the name of god Amen I William Shackspeare of Stratford vpon Avon in the countie of Warr gent in perfect health & memorie god be praysed doe make & Ordayne this my last will & testament in manner & forme followeing. That is to saye ffirst I Comend my Soule into the handes of god my Creator, hoping & assuredlie beleeving through thonelie merittes of Jesus Christe my Saviour to be made partaker of lyfe everlastinge, And my bodye to the Earth whereof yt ys made. Item I Gyve & bequeath vnto my daughter Judyth One Hundred & ffyftie poundes of lawfull English money to be paied vnto her . . . One Hundred **Poundes in discharge of her marriage porcion**

within one yeare after my deceas . . . & the ffyftie
poundes Residewe thereof vpon her Surrendring
of . . . All her estate & Right . . . in or to one
Copiehold tenemente . . . in Stratford vpon Avon
aforesaied in the saied countie of Warr, being
parcell or holden of the mannour of Rowington,
vnto my daughter Susanna Hall & her heires for
ever. Item I Gyve & bequeath vnto my saied
daughter Judith One Hundred & ffyftie Poundes
more if shee or Anie issue of her bodie be Lyvinge
att thend of three Yeares next ensueing the daie of
the date of this my will . . . And if she dye within
the saied terme without issue of her bodye then
my will ys & I doe gyve & bequeath One Hundred
Poundes thereof to my Neece [i.e. granddaughter]
Elizabeth Hall & the ffiftie Poundes to be sett
fourth by my executours during the lief of my
Sister Johane Harte & the vse & profitt thereof
Cominge shalbe payed to my saied Sister Jone, &
after her deceas the saied l^{li} shall Remaine
Amongst the children of my saied Sister Equallie
to be devided Amongst them. . . . Item I gyve &
bequeath vnto my saied sister Jone xx^{li} & all my
wearing Apparrell to be paied & deliuered within
one yeare after my deceas, And I doe will & devise
vnto her the house with thappurtenaunces in
Stratford wherein she dwelleth for her naturall
lief vnder the yearelie Rent of xij^{d}. Item I gyve &
bequeath vnto her three sonns Welliam Harte
[blank] Hart & Michaell Harte ffyve poundes A
peece to be payed within one Yeare after my deceas. Item I gyve & bequeath vnto the saied Elizabeth Hall All my Plate (except my brod silver &
gilt bole) that I now have att the date of this my
will. Item I gyve & bequeath vnto the Poore of
Stratford aforesaid tenn poundes, to m^{r} Thomas

Combe my Sword, to Thomas Russell Esquier ffyve
poundes, & to ffrauncis Collins of the Borough of
Warr in the countie of Warr gent thirteene
poundes Sixe shillinges & Eight pence to be paied
within one Yeare after my deceas. Item I gyve &
bequeath to Hamlett Sadler xxvj^s viij^d to buy him
A Ringe, to William Raynoldes gent xxvj^s viij^d to
buy him A Ringe, to my godson William Walker
xx^s in gold, to Anthonye Nashe gent xxvj^s viij^d, &
to Mr John Nashe xxvj^s viij^d, & to my ffellowes
John Hemynge Richard Burbage & Henry Cun-
dell xxvj^s viij^d A peece to buy them Ringes. Item
I Gyve Will bequeath & Devise vnto my daughter
Susanna Hall for better enabling of her to per-
forme this my will & towardes the performans
thereof All that Capitall Messuage or tenemente
with thappurtenaunces in Stratford aforesaied
Called the newe place wherein I nowe dwell &
twoe messuages or tenementes with thappurtenaunces scituat lyeing & being in Henley streete
within the borough of Stratford aforesaied, And
all my barnes stables Orchardes gardens landes tenementes & hereditamentes whatsoever scituat lyeing & being or to be had Receyved perceyved or
taken within the townes Hamlettes villages ffieldes
& groundes of Stratford vpon Avon Oldstratford
Bushopton & Welcombe or in anie of them in the
saied countie of Warr, And alsoe All that Messuage or tenemente with thappurtenaunces wherein one John Robinson dwelleth, scituat lyeing &
being in the blackfriers in London nere the Wardrobe, & all other my landes tenementes and hereditamentes whatsoever; To Have & to hold All &
singuler the saied premisses with their Appurten-
naunces vnto the saied Susanna Hall for & during
the terme of her naturall lief, & after her Deceas

to the first sonne of her bodie lawfullie yssueing
& to the heires Males of the bodie of the saied first
Sonne lawfullie yssueing, & for defalt of such issue
to the second Sonne of her bodie lawfullie issueing
and to the heires Males of the bodie of the saied
Second Sonne lawfullie yssueinge, & for defalt of
such heires to the third Sonne of the bodie of the
saied Susanna Lawfullie yssueing and of the heires
Males of the bodie of the saied third sonne lawfullie yssueing, And for defalt of such issue the
same soe to be & Remaine to the ffourth ffyfth
sixte & Seaventh sonnes of her bodie lawfullie issueing one after Another & to the heires Males of
the bodies of the said fourth fifth Sixte & Seaventh
sonnes lawfullie yssueing, in such manner as yt ys
before Lymitted to be & Remaine to the first second and third Sonns of her bodie & to their heires
Males; And for defalt of such issue the said premisses to be & Remaine to my sayed Neece Hall & the
heires males of her bodie Lawfullie yssueing, and
for defalt of issue to my daughter Judith & the
heires Males of her bodie lawfullie yssueing, And
for defalt of such issue to the Right heires of me
the saied William Shackspere for ever. Item I gyve
vnto my wief my second best bed with the furni-
ture Item I gyve & bequeath to my saied daughter
Judith my broad silver gilt bole. All the Rest of
my goodes chattels Leases plate Jewels & householde stuffe whatsoever, after my dettes and Lega-
sies paied & my funerall expences discharged, I
gyve devise & bequeath to my Sonne in Lawe John
Hall gent & my daughter Susanna his wief whom
I ordaine & make executours of this my Last will
and testament. And I doe intreat & Appoint the
saied Thomas Russell Esquier & ffrauncis Collins
gent to be overseers hereof. And doe Revoke All

former wills & publishe this to be my last will and testament. In witnesse whereof I have hereunto put my hand the daie & Yeare first aboue Written.

By me William Shakspeare.

witnes to the publishing
hereof. Fra: Collyns
Julyus Shawe
John Robinson
Hamnet Sadler
Robert Whattcott

The will bears a later statement that it was probated (i.e. it was demonstrated genuine, and proof of Shakespeare's death was presented) by his son-in-law John Hall on 22 June 1616. The witnesses were the lawyer who drew up the will and four Stratford neighbors. Thomas Russell, the overseer appointed to serve with Collins, had fairly extensive estates not far from Stratford. Though quite a little has been discovered about his life, nothing is known of his relationship with Shakespeare.

This document is a characteristic will of a man of property in the reign of James I. The pious opening comes from a popular book of forms for wills and other legal instruments prepared by a lawyer named William West. The provisions of the will show that Shakespeare was trying to set up conditions so that the bulk of his property would be held together for his descendants, first his daughter Susanna, then her eldest surviving son, and then that son's eldest surviving son, and so on. The estate he tried thus to hold together was principally New Place, the houses in Henley Street, land in Old Stratford, and the London property in Blackfriars. The fact that all four of his grandchildren died childless foiled his purpose and eventually broke up his estate.

The smaller bequests in the will are the discharge of obligations or the expressions of friendship and love. His sister and nephews are remembered; eight or nine Stratford friends are remembered; but from his long career in London he singles out only three persons, all three fellow actors, fellow theater owners, and members of the King's company: "my ffellowes John Hemynge Richard Burbage & Henry Cundell."

Many hundreds of pages have been written about this will—mostly by men who know little or nothing of the thousands of extant Jacobean wills, but who want to use this one to support their favorite inferences about the character and experience of the dramatist. Wills seldom provide such information. The usual Jacobean ones even ignore most of the personal property of the deceased unless a separate inventory has been preserved, and generally the inventory has been lost, as Shakespeare's has been, though it was shown to the court when the will was probated on the 22d of the following June. Only particular items requested to be taken out of the estate—like Shakespeare's sword for his friend Thomas Combe, or the wearing apparel for his sister Joan, or the broad silver-gilt bowl for his daughter, or the famous second-best bed for his wife— are ordinarily mentioned in wills. All the rest of the personal property, like books and manuscripts and household furnishings and rings and such, are not itemized but are lumped together in this will, as in most, in the phrase "All the Rest of my goodes chattels Leases plate Jewels & householde stuffe whatsoever." Rights in his plays and poems Shakespeare did not own and could not bequeath; they were the property of the dramatic company for which they had been written and of the publishers who had printed them. The manuscripts of his plays were also the property of the company; if Shakespeare still possessed early drafts or "foul papers," they would be included in the "goodes chattels . . . & householde stuffe" that were left to John and Susanna Hall.

Many romantic or lurid tales about Shakespeare and his wife have been told, inspired in part by the single and apparently slighting mention of Anne Shakespeare in the will. But in fact, in order to provide for his wife under the law of the time, it was not necessary for Shakespeare to mention her at all. By law the widow during her lifetime received the income from one-third of her husband's estate. Exceptions were sometimes made—for instance when equivalent provision for the wife's widowhood had previously been made in her marriage settlement; no such provision is known for Anne Shakespeare, however, and it is unlikely that there was one, since William and his father had comparatively little property with which to make a settlement at the time of the marriage. Dower rights—i.e. widow's inheritance—could also be eliminated in the original deed for a piece of property, but such provision is made in only one of Shakespeare's deeds, that for the Blackfriars house in London. Thus Anne Hathaway Shakespeare would have had an adequate income from one-third of her husband's rather considerable estate had she been ignored in the will entirely. The bequest of the second-best bed is a special additional remembrance, like the silver-gilt bowl for Judith. The reason for this particular bequest is not known. A house the size of New Place would have had a number of beds, and what the special association was with the second-best bed—or with any of the others—no one knows, though hundreds have urged their favorite guesses.

Four weeks after Shakespeare's will was revised by Francis Collins and witnessed by Julyus Shawe, John Robinson, Hamnet Sadler, and Robert Whattcott, the dramatist died. There is no contemporary record of the cause or the circumstances of his death. In 1662, however, a new vicar named John Ward came to Holy Trinity Church, Stratford, where he remained for about twenty years. This clergyman, who had some medical training and a great deal of medical interest, kept notebooks, or diaries, sixteen volumes of which are now in the Folger Shakespeare Library. Several of Ward's entries record information about the dramatist or his family which he must have heard in the town about fifty years after Shakespeare's death. Two of these diary entries read:

> Shakespear had but 2 daughters, one whereof M. Hall, ye physitian, married, and by her had one daughter, to wit, ye Lady Bernard of Abbingdon.

> Shakespear, Drayton, and Ben Jhonson, had a merry meeting, and itt seems drank too hard, for Shakespear died of a feavour there contracted.

The Reverend John Ward's story is not necessarily accurate, but at least he was in a better position to get the facts, or an echo of the facts, than anyone else who has written on the subject. The men mentioned in the second entry could well have had a "merry meeting" with the poet. The poet Michael Drayton was a Warwickshire man and a frequent visitor at the village of Clifford Chambers, two or three miles from Stratford; Ben Jonson was a friend of Shakespeare's, as his admiring and affectionate verses published in the Folio of 1623 show. But possibilities do not make a probability.

Two days after the date of death recorded on Shakespeare's monument, the registers of Holy Trinity Church record his burial, as they had recorded his christening and that of his children:

April 25   Will. Shakspere gent.

He was buried within the chancel of Holy Trinity, as prominent citizens often were in the parish churches of the time. Within a few years of his death there was erected, presumably by the family, the monument which is referred to in commendatory verses in the Folio of 1623. Seventeenth-century monuments to prominent parishioners in English parish churches were usually erected, as Shakespeare's was, not over the tomb but on a nearby wall, and it was often several years after the burial before they were in place.

The memorial which was placed on the wall near Shakespeare's tomb consists of a bust of the poet within a formal framework; he is shown writing with a quill pen. On either side of the bust are Corinthian columns; above are Shakespeare's arms, helm, and crest, two small nude figures representing Rest and Labor, and above all a skull. The design of the monument and the central figure of a man writing are not unlike other memorials of the time, most notably that of the historian John Stow, who died in 1605; his monument in the church of St. Andrew Undershaft in London shows the same arrangement of details and the same general position for the central figure, though the men portrayed do not look alike.

Shakespeare's monument was carved and erected by Gheerart Janssen (the name is often Anglicized as Gerrard Johnson); he was an Anglo-Flemish professional tomb-maker who lived in Southwark not far from the Globe Theatre. Janssen had also made the tomb of Shakespeare's friend John Combe, which stands a few feet away from his in the Stratford church. Like most effigies on tombs of the time, and like the statue of Hermione which Shakespeare described in *The Winter's Tale,* this one was designed to be painted in lifelike colors, and it was so painted by Janssen or his workmen, as shown by vestiges of the original colors still remaining. In time, of course, these colors wore off, and in the late eighteenth century when the style in tombs had changed, the monument was all painted white to look like stone, thus giving a flat appearance to the face. In 1861 the white paint was removed and the effigy painted in colors again, but one may doubt how close they are to Shakespeare's own. Indeed it is probable that Janssen's statue, though surely recognizable, was not wholly accurate, for the man was a tomb-maker, not a sculptor of genius, and it is even possible that he may never have seen the dramatist. But Shakespeare's wife, his two daughters, and his two sons-in-law were all living in Stratford when the monument was erected; presumably one or some of them—most likely Dr. John Hall—commissioned and paid for it, and we may guess that the resemblance to the dead poet, though not necessarily perfect, was acceptable.

At any rate this bust in Holy Trinity Church at Stratford and the engraving in the Folio of 1623 are the only likenesses of Shakespeare that have any claim at all to authenticity, though dozens of forged pictures, or misattributions, or romantic reconstructions have been brought forward from time to time and have been printed in many books and accepted by many thousands of the credulous.

The tablet under Janssen's bust bears the following inscription:

IVDICIO PYLIVM, GENIO SOCRATEM, ARTE MARONEM:
TERRA TEGIT, POPVLVS MAERET, OLYMPVS HABET.

STAY PASSENGER, WHY GOEST THOV BY SO FAST?
READ IF THOV CANST, WHOM ENVIOVS DEATH
   HATH PLAST,
WITH IN THIS MONVMENT SHAKSPEARE: WITH
   WHOME,

QVICK NATVRE DIDE: WHOSE NAME DOTH DECK
    YS TOMBE,
FAR MORE THEN COST: SIEH   ALL, YT HE HATH
    WRITT,
LEAVES LIVING ART, BVT PAGE, TO SERVE HIS WITT.

Better known than this inscription are the lines
which are carved on the slab of stone which covers the
grave itself:

    GOOD FREND FOR IESVS SAKE FORBEARE,
    TO DIGG THE DVST ENCLOASED HEARE!
    BLESTE BE YE MAN YT SPARES THES STONES,
    AND CVRST BE HE YT MOVES MY BONES.

This well-known verse, possibly written by Shakespeare himself, is not directed to the occasional passer-
by, as are most epitaphs, including the one on the wall
monument; it is directed to the sexton of the church
and his successors, and it is phrased to appeal to sextons. In old parish churches, like the Stratford one,
where respected parishioners had been buried under
the church floor for several centuries (and continued
to be for about two centuries more), the sexton un-
avoidably disturbed the bones in the old graves when
he dug new ones in the same spot, just as the grave-
digger did in the fifth act of *Hamlet*. Beside the parish
church at Stratford, as at many churches in the time,
there was a charnel house, now demolished, where the
bones from old graves were thrown when they were
removed to make room for new bodies. The inscription
on Shakespeare's grave is designed to frighten off future
sextons casually engaged in such desecration.

After the dramatist's death his family continued to
live at New Place as he had planned, but in diminish-
ing numbers. On 8 August 1623 the parish burial registers record the interment of his wife in the laconic

entry, "Mrs Shakspeare." Her grave, beside that of the dramatist in the chancel of the church, bears the inscription:

> Heere Lyeth Interred The Body Of Anne Wife Of William Shakespeare Who Departed This Life The 6th Day of Avgvst: 1623. Being Of The Age Of·67·Yeares.

A six-line Latin epitaph follows.

On 26 November 1635 the parish burial registers have an entry for Shakespeare's son-in-law:

> Johannes Hall, medicus peritissimus.

The parish clerk's unusual designation of "medicus peritissimus," most skillful physician, suggests the great respect for Dr. Hall in the town. He was also buried in the chancel of the church beside the grave in which his wife Susanna was later interred. Hall's gravestone also records his Shakespeare connection:

> . . . Hee Marr: Svsanna, Y^e Daughter & Coheir, of Will: Shakespeare, Gent.

Shakespeare's grandsons Thomas and Richard Quiney were buried from the parish church in 1639; Thomas Nash, the first husband of his granddaughter Elizabeth, was buried in the grave next to Shakespeare's in 1647. Susanna Hall was buried next to her husband in 1649. Judith was buried in 1662, but the location of her grave is unknown.

Shakespeare's last surviving descendant, his granddaughter Elizabeth Hall Nashe Bernard, appears to have lived at New Place until after her marriage in 1649 to John (later Sir John) Bernard. She died at Abington in February 1670 and in her will bequeathed New Place outside the Shakespeare family. It no longer exists. About the end of the seventeenth century the house was rebuilt, and in 1759 the then owner, the Reverend Francis Gastrell, in a quarrel with the town of Stratford had the house demolished.

With Lady Bernard's death the Shakespeare family disappears from Stratford after more than a century of prominence in the town, and their great house of New Place is gone, but the Henley Street houses and many other buildings familiar to them, their graves, and many documents recording their activities remain as tokens of the long and intimate association of William Shakespeare, his parents, his children, and his grandchildren with the town of Stratford-upon-Avon.

CHAPTER 3

In London

THOUGH it is apparent that Shakespeare ordinarily considered himself to be a Stratford man and his close associations with his native town were continuous, his great achievements were made in London, where all the permanent playhouses were found. Professionally he was a man of the theater, and it was in the London theater that his genius was lavished. His activities as actor and as playwright may be most illuminatingly considered separately in later chapters, but there are records of Shakespeare's life in London which are not theatrical.

When he first arrived in the capital or how he happened to come, no one has yet discovered, though there have been copious guesses. The gap in our knowledge of his career extends, as we have seen, from the record of the baptism of the twins Hamnet and Judith at Holy Trinity, Stratford, in February 1585 to the first allusion to his London activities in 1592, the so-called Lost Years. We have noticed the possibilities that in these

Lost Years he may have taught in a school or have been a provincial actor, but these two suggestions are only the most plausible of the many speculations or traditions about the period of seven years between his disappearance from the Stratford records and his known residence in London. He was firmly established in London by the late summer of 1592, when he was well enough known to be castigated in a pamphlet by the jealous Robert Greene, and by 1594 he was a member of the Lord Chamberlain's company, but both these facts belong in our later discussion of Shakespeare the Actor. We are concerned here only with those aspects of his life in London which are not directly connected with the theater.

The first nondramatic fact concerns his residence. From 1594 through 1597 the Lord Chamberlain's men were performing part of the time at the playhouse called simply The Theatre, part of the time at the Curtain, and part of the time at the Cross Keys Inn. The Theatre and the Curtain were located close together a few hundred yards north of Bishopsgate outside the city proper, and the Cross Keys Inn was in Gracious Street (or Grace Church Street) near the heart of the city. About half way between these two playing areas, in the parish of St. Helen's Bishopsgate and about a ten-minute walk from either The Theatre or the Cross Keys, Shakespeare is first found residing in London. The records which give us this information consist of the reports of tax collectors; they are not specific about the period of his residence, but they imply that in November 1597 Shakespeare had recently moved to Southwark after having lived for a time in St. Helen's parish.

The tax gatherers for this district reported in November 1597 on their collections of the second installment of a tax assessed in October 1596. They said that within the warde of Byshopsgate London . . . the persons herevnder named are all ether dead, departed, and gone out of the sayde warde or their goodes soe eloigned or conveyd out of the same or in suche a pryvate or coverte manner kept . . . [that] the sayde secound payment of the sayde last subsydye nether mighte nor coulde by anye meanes by them the sayde petty collectors, or ether of them, be levyed of them . . .

St Ellen's parishe

Peter Dallila	l^{li}	l^s
William Shackspere	v^{li}	v^s
Thomas Stythe	xxx^{li}	xxx^s
William Boyese	xxx^{ll}	xxx^s

About a year later Shakespeare was again assessed on another tax in the parish of St. Helen's. This time the assessed rate was more than double, though the property evaluation was the same. Again the collectors said that they were unable to collect, as they indicated by placing opposite Shakespeare's name and a number of others in the list the abbreviation "Affid" (for affidavit: that is, the collectors swear that they have tried to collect but have been unable to do so).

Affid   William Shakespeare   v^{li} xiij^s iiij^d

Shakespeare's name was then entered with a number of others in a long list of defaulters of various parishes who had no goods in the parish for distraint.

In Warda de Bishopsgate . . . In parochia Sancte Helene . . . Willelmus Shakespeare ibidem xiij^s iiij^d

On 6 October 1599 he was again entered in a list of persons still owing taxes, but though he was listed for the parish of St. Helen's Bishopsgate, additional notes indicated that he was found to have moved across the river to Surrey.

> Willelmus Shakspeare in parochia sancte Helene in Warda predicta debet xiij^s iiij^d. de eodem subsidio ibidem [Added later] Respondebit in rotulo sequente in Residuum Sussex. [William Shakespeare in the parish of Saint Helen in the Ward aforesaid owes 13s. 4d. of the same subsidy there. He answers in the following roll in Residuum Sussex]

And finally a year later, on 6 October 1600, the same arrears are entered for "Willelmus Shakspeare in parochia sancte Helene," but they are entered on the roll for the county of Sussex (of which, for tax purposes, Surrey was considered a part), and marginal notes apparently indicate that they were transferred to the Bishop of Winchester, who administered the area in Surrey near the Globe Theatre called the Liberty of the Clink. Further marginal notes seem to indicate that the taxes were finally paid to the Bishop or to his agent.

These tax records of Elizabethan London are not easy to follow, but the most probable reconstruction of the facts which the records represent is that before 1596 Shakespeare was living in the parish of St. Helen's Bishopsgate, but that he had left the parish when the collectors made their rounds some time before November 1597 and they could therefore not collect. Eventually the collectors found that he had moved across the river to the London suburb on the Bankside. His name was accordingly transferred to the jurisdiction of the Liberty of the Clink, where the tax was eventually collected.

Other evidence confirms this move across the river to the newer theater district in Southwark, of which the

Liberty of the Clink was a part. The great eighteenth-century scholar Edmond Malone, who saw many documents that have subsequently been lost, wrote in 1796:

> From a paper now before me, which formerly belonged to Edward Alleyn, the player, our poet appears to have lived in Southwark near the Bear-Garden, in 1596. Another curious document in my possession . . . affords the strongest presumptive evidence that he continued to reside in Southwark to the year 1608.

Shakespeare's residence in the theater district on the Bankside is also indicated in another nontheatrical record of his London life. In Michaelmas term (early October through November) of 1596, an entry for sureties of the peace concerning Shakespeare and several others was made in the Controlment Rolls of the Court of Queen's Bench. Expanded and translated from its highly abbreviated Latin, the record reads:

> England   Be it known that William Wayte craves sureties of the peace against William Shakspare, Francis Langley, Dorothy Soer, wife of John Soer, and Anne Lee, for fear of death, and so forth.
> Writ of attachment issued to the sheriff of Surrey, returnable on the eighteenth of St. Martin [i.e. 29 November 1596]

The fact that this writ was issued to the sheriff of Surrey indicates again Shakespeare's residence in his bailiwick—that is, across the river in Surrey. A writ like this one was a common device in Elizabethan quarrels; Shakespeare's father had had one issued against four Stratford men fourteen years before. One party (in this case William Wayte) went to court and stated that he was afraid of attack by the other parties (in this case

William Shakespeare, Francis Langley, Dorothy Soer, and Anne Lee). The court then issued a warrant to the sheriff of the district to arrest the persons complained against or to take their bond that they would not injure the plaintiff. The procedure was exceedingly common at the time, and usually one can tell very little now about the justice of the complaints. Often, indeed, they were a form of retaliation, and it was the plaintiff himself who had previously been justly complained against by one or more of the parties he now accused. Something of the sort may well have happened in this case, for it is suggestive that just a few weeks before William Wayte made his complaint against Francis Langley and the others, the court had recorded that "Francis Langley craves sureties of the peace against William Gardener and William Wayte for fear of death, and so forth."

Nothing is known of the details of the dispute or of its cause. The identities of the parties are, however, again suggestive. The two women are unknown, but Francis Langley was the builder and owner of the Swan Theatre, which had been built just a year or two before in Paris Garden on the Bankside in the county of Surrey. William Wayte was the stepson of William Gardiner, a wealthy and widely hated justice of the peace of very dubious character. Mountains of conjecture have been reared on these documents, on others showing the doubtful dealings of William Gardiner with other unrelated persons, and on certain characters in Shakespeare's *Henry IV, Part 2* and *The Merry Wives of Windsor,* especially Shallow, who is alleged to be a caricature of Justice William Gardiner. The association of the names of William Shakespeare and Francis Langley has made plausible the suggestion that Shakespeare and his fellows of the Lord Chamberlain's company were acting at this time in Langley's new Swan Theatre. All we know certainly from these documents, however, is that Shakespeare was living in Surrey in November 1596, that he was in some way associated with Francis Langley, builder and owner of the Swan Theatre, and that William Wayte had something against the two of them and Dorothy Soer and Anne Lee.

Where Shakespeare lived in London during the next few years we cannot be sure. The Bankside, where Malone's now lost documents seemed to show that he lived until 1608, would have been a convenient residence, for the Globe Theatre, erected there early in 1599, was the center of all his dramatic activities for the next ten years. At some time in this period, however, Shakespeare lived in another part of town with a French Huguenot family named Mountjoy. Incidentally it is noteworthy that there are never any records of Shakespeare's wife and children in London; apparently they stayed in Stratford while he acted and wrote in the city.

The Mountjoys were tire-makers—that is, they created the elaborate structures of gold, silver, and jewels which great ladies wore in their hair; in at least one instance the Mountjoys made one of their creations for the Queen of England. They lived in the northwest part of the city, about half-way between St. Paul's Cathedral and Cripplegate, and for a time—at least in 1604, and perhaps before and after—Shakespeare lived with them. Our knowledge of this residence and of Shakespeare's French friends comes from a law suit brought several years later, in 1612, against Christopher Mountjoy by his son-in-law and former apprentice, Stephen Belott.

Belott claimed that when he had married Mary Mountjoy on 19 November 1604, Christopher Mountjoy, her father, had promised to give £60 as her portion, and that he promised further to leave her £200 more in his will. Both these promises, Belott alleged, had been broken. In testimony to the original agreement about the dowry, the attorneys in the suit called a number of witnesses, one of whom was William Shakespeare.

The testimony of witnesses was not taken in seventeenth-century trials as it is now. The usual custom then was for the attorneys to agree on a series of questions, or "interrogatories," which were then asked of all witnesses. The replies to the interrogatories—the depositions—were set down in writing and signed by the witnesses. The depositions of several witnesses in the Belott-Mountjoy suit, including that of William Shakespeare, afford us some knowledge of Shakespeare's nonprofessional life in London.

Joan Johnson, formerly a maid in the Mountjoy household, testified on 11 May 1612 that Mrs. Mountjoy encouraged the affair between her daughter Mary and her husband's apprentice, Stephen Belott:

> And as she remembereth the defendant [i.e. Christopher Mountjoy] did send and perswade one Mr Shakespeare that laye in the house to perswade the plaintiff [Stephen Belott] to the same marriadge.

On the same day another witness, Daniel Nicholas, testified that

> he herd one Wm: Shakespeare saye that the defendant did beare a good opinion of the plaintiff and affected him well when he served him, and did move the plaintiff by him the said Shakespeare to haue [a] marriadge betweene his daughter Marye Mountioye [and] the plaintiff, and for that purpose sent him the said Sh[akespeare] to the plaintiff to perswade the plaintiff to the same, as Shakespere tould him this deponent, which was effected and

solempnized vppon promise of a porcion with her
. . . the plaintiff did requeste him this deponent to
goe with his wyffe to Shakespe[are] to vnderstande
the truthe howe muche and what the defendant
did promise to bestowe on his daughter in marriadge with him the plaintiff, who did soe. And
askinge Shakespeare therof, he answered that he
promissed yf the plaintiff would marrye with
Marye his the defendantes onlye daughter, he the
defendant would by his promise as he remembered
geue the plaintiff with her in marriadge about the
some of ffyftye poundes in money and certayne
houshould stuffe.

In a later deposition, on 19 June 1612, Daniel Nicholas further testified that

M[r]: William Shakespeare tould him this deponent
that the defendant sent him the said M[r] Shakespeare to the plaintiff about suche a marriadge to
be hadd betweene them, and Shakespeare tould
this deponent that the defendant tould him that
yf the plaintiff would marrye the said Marye his
daughter he would geue him the plaintiff a some
of monney with her for a porcion in marriadge
with her . . . Wherevppon, and in regard M[r]
Shakespeare hadd tould them that they should
haue a some of monney for a porcion from the
father, they weare made suer by M[r] Shakespeare
by geuinge there consent, and agreed to marrye,
[geuinge eache others hand to the hande *deleted*]
and did marrye.

On the same day William Eaton testified to much
the same effect as to what "M[r] Shakespeare" had told
him about the arrangement of the marriage, and No-

well Mountjoy testified that Belott had told him that "Mr Shakespeare" was engaged by Mountjoy to help arrange the marriage. On 11 May 1612 Shakespeare himself testified about his part in bringing the parties together.

William Shakespeare of Stratford vpon Aven in the Countye of Warwicke gentleman of the age of xlviij yeres or thereaboutes . . . sayethe he knowethe the partyes plaintiff and deffendant and hathe know[ne] them bothe.as he now remembrethe for the space of tenne yeres or thereaboutes . . . he did know the complainant when he was servant with the deffendant, and that . . . he verely thinkethe that the said complainant was a very good and industrious servant in the said service . . . and that he [Shakespeare] hath hard the deffendant and his wyefe diuerse and sundry tymes saye and reporte that the said complainant was a very honest fellow: . . . And further this deponent sayethe that the said deffendantes wyeffe did sollicitt and entreat this deponent to move and perswade the said complainant to effect the said marriadge, and accordingly this deponent did moue and perswade the complainant thervnto: . . . this deponent sayth that the defendant promissed to geue the said complainant a porcion in marriadg[e] with Marye his daughter, but what certayne porcion he rememberethe not, nor when to be payed, nor knoweth that the defendant promissed the plaintiff twoe hundered poundes with his daughter Marye at the tyme of his decease. But sayth that the plaintiff was dwellinge with the defendant in his house, and they had amongeste them selues manye conferences about there marriadge which [afterwardes] was consumated and solempnized.

Several facts about the dramatist and his London life emerge from the testimony in this suit. Since he identified himself for the London court on 11 May 1612 as William Shakespeare of Stratford-upon-Avon, he had evidently at that time no London residence and had presumably retired to Stratford, making only occasional trips to London. He had known the Mountjoys and Belott for about ten years and, according to Joan Johnson's testimony, had been lodging with them before the wedding in November 1604. From other sources we know that in 1612 Mountjoy lived near St. Olave's church in the northwest corner of London, and presumably he had been there eight years earlier when Shakespeare was a member of the household. The dramatist's residence with the family would have been from about 1602 at least until the wedding in November 1604, and perhaps longer, and during these years he was evidently the family's trusted friend who helped to arrange the marriage and even, according to Daniel Nicholas, supervised the betrothal. What effect this intimacy with a family of French Huguenots had on Shakespeare's thought and knowledge is a matter for pleasant speculation. His most extensive treatment of the French, in the *Henry VI* plays and *Henry V*, gives us no clue, for these plays were written from three to ten or more years before 1602, the date he indicates for his first acquaintance with the Mountjoys.

A different kind of record offers the possibility that Shakespeare was at St. Saviour's Church in Southwark in 1607. On the last day of that year an actor named Edmund Shakespeare was buried at this church near London Bridge, the church of the parish in which the Globe Theatre was located. The dramatist had a younger brother named Edmund, who had been baptized at Stratford on 3 May 1580, and probably the actor buried was the younger brother who had followed the poet to London and entered his profession. Both the profession and the parish suggest a possible protégé of the dramatist, but unfortunately we have no corroborating evidence beyond the name and the appropriate dates. The first London record of Edmund Shakespeare is found in the burial registers of St. Giles Cripplegate under the date 12 August 1607:

> Edward sonne of Edward Shackspeere,
> Player, base-borne

Later, on 31 December of the same year, the interment of the actor himself is recorded in the burial registers of St. Saviour's Southwark:

> Edmond Shakespeare a player in the Church

and another entry is found in the fee book of the church:

> 31 Edmond Shakspeare a player buried in the Church, with a forenoone knell of the great bell,   xx[s]

The last two records certainly refer to the same man, and it is very likely that the first one from St. Giles Cripplegate refers to him as well. The difference between Edmund and Edward was not very significant for the parish clerk at St. Giles Cripplegate, who, in other entries in his register, makes no distinction between Jone and Joanna, Eleanor and Helen, Orton and Horton, Morgan and Martin, and Shanbrooke and Shambrooke. The rather large fee paid for Edmund's burial and funeral knell show that someone of means was interested in him; it could well have been the dramatist whose theater was nearby.

These are the last records of Shakespeare's nonprofessional life in London before he retired to Stratford, some time before 11 May 1612. But he continued to have dealings in London, and he evidently came back to town occasionally, as he did to testify in the Belott-Mountjoy suit.

In 1613 he is recorded in an activity which is most unfamiliar and perhaps seems unsuitable to modern readers. During the reigns of Elizabeth and James the great nobles frequently staged tourneys or tilts, which were somewhat debased forms of the old knightly tournaments of the Middle Ages. There were specially built tiltyards at Whitehall, Hampton Court, and Greenwich where tilting took place with some frequency and always on the anniversary of the succession; for James I this date was 24 March. It was customary for the great nobles who tilted as challengers or as defendants to have special insignia prepared for their shields—emblems with mottoes which made cryptic allusions to the qualities or hopes or resolves of the bearer. These tourney shields were conspicuously displayed for the spectators at the tilt, and some of them were preserved for years in the shield gallery at Whitehall Palace. One of the noble contenders in the tourney at court on 24 March 1613, which celebrated the accession of James I, was the Earl of Rutland. He had the emblem and motto for his special shield designed by Shakespeare and the painting done by Shakespeare's colleague and friend, the great actor Richard Burbage, who was also an amateur painter. The facts were recorded a week or two after the tilt in the accounts of the Earl's steward at Belvoir Castle:

> Item, 31 Martii, to Mr Shakspeare in gold about my Lorde's impreso, xliiijs; to Richard Burbage for paynting and making yt, in gold xliiijs.——iiijli. viijs.

At about the same time as his work for the Earl of Rutland, Shakespeare was concerned in a London real estate transaction not unlike those in which he was involved at Stratford. He bought a house in Blackfriars not far from the Blackfriars Theatre in which his company then acted in the winter months and in which he was a principal stockholder. Both the theater and Shakespeare's new purchase had once been parts of the huge old Dominican (or Blackfriars) priory which had passed into private hands when all English monastic establishments were abolished at the Reformation. Presumably Shakespeare bought the Blackfriars house as an investment; there is no suggestion that he ever intended to live in it. Two copies of the deed recording the transaction are extant: one is Shakespeare's copy signed by Henry Walker, the seller, a document now at the Folger Shakespeare Library in Washington; and the other, in the same words, is Walker's copy, signed by Shakespeare and two of his three trustees; it is now preserved in the Guildhall in London. Walker's copy of the deed reads:

This Indenture made the tenthe day of Marche, in the yeare of our Lord God, according to the computacion of the church of England, one thowsand six hundred and twelve [i.e. 1613 in the modern calendar] . . . Between Henry Walker citizein and Minstrell of London of th' one partie; And William Shakespeare of Stratford Vpon Avon in the countie of Warwick gentleman, William Johnson, citizein and Vintener of London, John Jackson and John Hemmyng of London gentlemen, of th' other partie; Witnesseth that the said Henry Walker (for and in consideracion of the somme of one hundred and fortie poundes of lawfull money of England to him in hande before th' ensealing hereof by the said William Shakespeare well & trulie paid, whereof and wherewith hee the said

Henry Walker doth acknowledge himselfe fullie satisfied and contented, and thereof, and of every part and parcell thereof doth cleerlie acquite and discharge the saide William Shakespeare, his heires, executours, administratours and assignes, and every of them by theis presentes) hath bargayned and soulde and by theis presentes doth fullie, cleerlie, and absolutlie bargayne and sell vnto the said William Shakespeare, William Johnson, John Jackson, and John Hemming, their heires, and assignes forever; All that dwelling house or Tenement with th' appurtenaunces situate and being within the Precinct, circuit and compasse of the late black Fryers, London . . . And further that all and every fyne and fynes to bee levyed, recoveryes to bee suffered, estates and assurances at any tyme or tymes hereafter to bee had, made, executed, or passed by, or betweene the said parties of the premisses, or of any parcell thereof, shalbee, and shalbee esteemed, adiudged, deemed, and taken to bee to th' onlie and proper vse and behoofe of the said William Shakespeare his heires, and assignes forever, and to none other vse, intent or purpose. In witnesse whereof the said parties to theis Indentures interchaungablie have sett their seales. Yeoven the day and yeares first above written.

William Shakspē   Wᵐ Johnsonn   Jo: Jacksonn

As the wording of this document indicates, Shakespeare was the real purchaser of the property, for he alone is named as paying the purchase price, and it is to Shakespeare that all the rights of the property are assigned. Apparently the three others were added as trustees for Shakespeare. John Heminges was Shakespeare's long-time friend and associate as a Fellow of the King's company, one of the two men who later supervised the collection of his plays in the Folio of 1623. William Johnson was the host of the Mermaid, a celebrated London tavern with literary associations. John Jackson was a well-to-do London gentleman. As his trustees "in performance of the confidence and trust in them reposed by William Shakespeare," the three men sold the property about two years after Shakespeare's death.

The day following the sealing of the deed for the Blackfriars house, Shakespeare mortgaged the property back to Henry Walker for £60.

This Indenture made the eleventh day of Marche . . . Betweene William Shakespeare, of Stratford vpon Avon in the countie of Warwick, gentleman, William Johnson, citizein and Vintener of London, John Jackson and John Hemmyng, of London, gentlemen, of th' one partie, and Henry Walker, citizein and Minstrell of London, of th' other partie; Witnesseth that the said William Shakespeare, William Johnson, John Jackson and John Hemmyng, have dimised, graunted and to ferme letten, and by theis presentes doe dimise graunt, and to ferme lett vnto the said Henry Walker, All that dwelling house or Tenement . . . Prouided alwayes that if the said William Shakespeare, his heires, executours, administratours or assignes, or any of them, doe well and trulie paie or cause to bee paid to the said Henry Walker . . . the some of threescore poundes of lawfull money of England in and vpon the nyne and twentith day of September next comming after the date hereof . . . at one entier payment without delaie; That then and from thensforth this presente lease, dismise and graunt . . . shall cease, de-

termyne, and bee vtterlie voyde, frustrate, and of
none effect, as though the same had never beene
had ne made, theis presentes, or any thing therein
conteyned to the contrary . . . notwithstanding . . .
In witnesse whereof the said parties to these Indentures interchaungablie have sett their seales.
Yeoven the day and yeares first aboue written.
1612.

    Wᵐ Shakspẽ   Wᵐ Johnson   Jo: Jackson

Evidently Shakespeare paid for this new piece of property with £80 in cash and a mortgage for £60 as se-
curity for the balance. The later history of the property
would indicate that the mortgage was paid off when it
fell due.

About two years after the purchase Shakespeare was
a party to a friendly suit involving this Blackfriars
house and adjacent holdings. At the death of Anne
Bacon, who had owned Blackfriars property, a number
of deeds, charters, letters patent, etc., concerning the
several properties had passed into the hands of Anne's
son and heir, Matthew Bacon, who did not own any
of the property in question but needed a court order
to turn over to the owners the deeds and papers he had
inherited. A suit to that end was instituted in Chancery
on 26 April 1615 by

> Sir Thomas Bendishe Baronet, Edward Newport
> and Willyam Thoresbie Esquiours, Robert Dor-
> mer Esquiour and Marie his wife, Willyam Shake-
> spere, gent., and Richard Bacon Citezen of Lon-
> don.

Since Matthew Bacon in his reply admitted that he did
not own the property and expressed his willingness to
dispose of the papers as the court directed, on 22 May
1615 the court ordered him to deliver the papers to the

86

court for transfer to the proper parties. Presumably the court then delivered such of the papers as related to their property to Shakespeare and his associates in the friendly suit.

This document is the last record of Shakespeare's nonprofessional activities in London. It is evident that some time before 11 May 1612, when he testified for his friend Stephen Belott in the Belott-Mountjoy suit, he had moved back to Stratford and no longer considered himself a London resident.

These London business and legal records of the dramatist as a resident of the capital exhibit only his secondary interests. They record some of his places of residence, his occasional involvement in disputes, and his investments in real estate in London, made, as were the ones in the vicinity of Stratford, as part of his endeavor to build up an estate for his family. His primary activity in London was theatrical, and when we turn to his London career as actor, theater owner, and playwright, we approach what was clearly the absorbing interest of his life.

CHAPTER 4

The Actor

SHAKESPEARE'S first association with the theater appears to have been that of an actor in a regular repertory company, and the normal character of such an organization provides the background for his actions and for his methods as a playwright.

All professional acting in Shakespeare's time was in the hands of permanent repertory companies—at least the actors of each troupe hoped and intended that their company would be permanent. But in the theater at any period financial returns are always precarious, and most Elizabethan and Jacobean dramatic companies went bankrupt in a few years. Only three or four of them lasted as long as twenty years; only Shakespeare's company continued for nearly half a century.

In its general organization, the repertory company to which Shakespeare belonged—called the Lord Chamberlain's company at first; after May 1603 called the King's company—was, like its competitors, made up of three groups of men and boys. The most important group consisted of the senior actors who had contributed capital to the company, who took the princi-

pal roles, and who participated in the management of
the enterprise. These senior men were sometimes called
"sharers" because they held stock in the enterprise and
shared in the profits, and sometimes "fellows" of the
company. Shakespeare used both terms in their professional sense in *Hamlet,* Act III, Scene 2, when—
after the performance of the play of *The Mousetrap*
with the additions written by Hamlet has broken down
King Claudius in the presence of the court, and when
all but Hamlet and his friend Horatio have left the
stage—Hamlet waves his manuscript and says,

> Would not this, sir . . . get me a fellowship in a
> cry of players, sir?

And Horatio replies sourly, "Half a share."

Shakespeare again used one of these terms in the professional actor's sense in his will, in which he left rings
to three of the men who had been his colleagues for
more than twenty years as senior members or sharers
of the Lord Chamberlain-King's company:

> & to my ffellowes John Hemynge Richard Burbage
> & Henry Cundell xxvj^s viij^d A peece to buy them
> Ringes.

The group of sharers in a company varied in size
according to the prosperity of the enterprise. In Shakespeare's own company the number of sharers increased
from five in the earliest days to twelve at the time of
his death. In the eyes of the law these men *were* the
company, and the other actors were their employees.
Since the royal patent, or license, authorizing the company commonly listed the names of the sharers, they
were also sometimes called "patented members" (see
below, pp. 91–92).

The second group in the usual Elizabethan repertory
company was called the hired men. They were minor

actors and other functionaries in the theater who had invested no capital and who did not share in the profits but were paid weekly wages by the sharers. Among the hired men were musicians, stage managers, wardrobe keepers, and prompters, as well as minor actors.

The third group was made up of boys. Because there were no women on the professional English stage in Shakespeare's time or for forty years after his death, all the roles of women and children in his plays and in all the plays of his contemporaries were written to be performed by boys whose voices had not yet changed and who were highly trained in female impersonation. There were never very many of them in the company; they required extensive training, and their period of usefulness was necessarily limited. Plays of the time are written with comparatively few women's roles—usually no more than would require two or three boys after a little doubling had been arranged. Probably few companies kept more than six boys, several of whom would not be far enough advanced in their training to handle more than walk-on roles in a play.

In Shakespeare's time in London there was also a completely different type of dramatic company which was made up entirely of boys. For a time such boy companies, often called children's companies, were serious rivals of Shakespeare's troupe (he alludes to their competition in *Hamlet*), but since Shakespeare himself never wrote for a boy company and is not known ever to have had anything to do with one, the characteristics peculiar to this kind of organization can be ignored in considering his career.

Companies of professional actors were astonishingly numerous in England during the reigns of Queen Elizabeth and James I—far more numerous in proportion to the population than they are now. There were companies which played only in the provinces, but the important troupes, those for which nearly all the Elizabethan and Jacobean plays were written, were the great companies acting in their regular theaters in London and going on tour for only short periods in the year or when there were difficulties in London. In a strictly regulated state like Elizabethan and Jacobean England, these London companies were all licensed as the servants of some great nobleman; after 1603 they were licensed as servants of some member of the royal family. During Shakespeare's Lost Years, 1585–92, at sometime in which he first came to the capital, the principal London repertory companies were called Queen Elizabeth's Men, the Lord Admiral's Men, the Earl of Leicester's Men, and the Lord Chamberlain's Men. There were others, but these were the chief.

Each company received a patent as an acting organization, a document giving it royal sanction. Most of these patents for acting companies are now lost, but fourteen of them are still extant. A good example—though it is several years ahead of our story at the moment—is the one which was issued to Shakespeare's company by the new king in 1603. It is enrolled in the official patent rolls of the kingdom, now housed in the Public Record Office in London.

Com[missio] sp[ec]ial[is] p[ro] Laurencio ffletcher & Will[elm]o Shackespeare et al[iis]./

Iames by the grace of god &c' To all Iustices Maiors Sheriffes Constables hedborowes and other our Officers and louinge Subiectes greetinge knowe yee that Wee of our speciall grace certeine knowledge & mere motion haue licenced and aucthorized and by theise p'sentes doe licence and aucthorize theise our Servauntes lawrence ffletcher Will[ia]m Shake-

speare Richard Burbage Augustyne Phillippes
Iohn heninges henrie Condell Will[ia]m Sly Rob-
[er]t Armyn Richard Cowly and the rest of theire
Assosiates freely to vse and exercise the Arte and
faculty of playinge Comedies Tragedies histories
Enterludes moralls pastoralls Stageplaies and
Suche others like as theie haue alreadie studied or
hereafter shall vse or studie aswell for the recrea-
tion of our lovinge Subjectes as for our Solace and
pleasure when wee shall thincke good to see them
duringe our pleasure   And the said Commedies
tragedies histories Enterludes Morralles Pastoralls
Stageplayes and suche like to shewe and exercise
publiquely to theire best Commoditie when the in-
fection of the plague shall decrease aswell within
theire nowe vsual howse called the Globe within
our County of Surrey as alsoe within anie towne
halls or Moute halls or other conveniente places
within the lib[er]ties and freedome of anie other
Cittie vniversitie towne or Boroughe whatsoever
within our said Realmes and domynions willinge
and Commaundinge you and everie of you as you
tender our pleasure not onelie to p[er]mitt and
suffer them herein without anie your lettes hin-
drances or molestacions during our said pleasure
but alsoe to be aidinge and assistinge to. them yf
anie wronge be to them offered   And to allowe
them such former Curtesies as hath bene given to
men of theire place and quallitie and alsoe what
further favour you shall shewe to theise our Servauntes for our sake wee shall take kindlie at your
handes. In wytnesse whereof &c' witnesse our selfe
at westm[inster] the nyntenth day of May

This patent, though it belongs to a later stage in
Shakespeare's career, is the sort of document under

which the company by which he was first employed had to operate. How he became attached to such a company, just when he joined, or what he did for them at first are all unknown, a part of the Lost Years. It is most likely that he began as a hired man. There are several legends about his beginnings in the theater, but none has much to support it.

It was the practice of the London companies to present a different play nearly every day, somewhat as a modern opera company does, except that their repertory was much larger. They brought out new plays as often as they could get them and the rest of the time repeated old favorites, so that in any given month as many as ten or fifteen different plays might be acted, allowing for a number of repetitions, but seldom more than two or three consecutive performances of the same play. Under this system Shakespeare, or any other hired man, might well act in as many as fifty or sixty different plays in the course of a year. Such training was very strenuous, but it helped young actors to learn their profession more thoroughly than most modern ones can. Through some training of this sort the young man from Stratford must have been going during at least part of the Lost Years.

The earliest document attesting to Shakespeare's activity in London as actor and dramatist by its very nature implies that he had been acting and writing plays for some little time. It comes from the pen of a jealous rival playwright, Robert Greene. Greene was a Bohemian character of prodigious energy who in his short life poured out plays, romances, pamphlets, and poems enough to fill fifteen sizable volumes in a modern edition. Many of the details of his interesting and dissolute life are recorded, probably with some exaggeration, in his own pamphlets. Greene was one of a small minority of London playwrights in the 1580's and

93

1590's who, as university men, felt themselves some-what above the ruck of working writers. To some of these "University Wits" (Robert Greene, Thomas Nashe, Christopher Marlowe, George Peele, and Thomas Lodge), Greene addressed a section of a pamphlet written on his death-bed when he was destitute and nearly friendless. This pamphlet was entered for publication in the Stationers' Register on 20 September 1592, two and one-half weeks after the author's death, and is entitled *Greenes Groats-worth of Wit bought with a million of Repentance. Describing the follie of youth, the falshood of makeshift flatterers . . . Written before his death and published at his dyeing request.*

Toward the end of the pamphlet the embittered Greene addresses his friends, the other University Wits who have been writing for the dramatic companies, to warn them against the actors and particularly against the actor-dramatist William Shakespeare.

> *To those Gentlemen his Quondam acquaintance, that spend their wits in making plaies, R. G. wisheth a better exercise, and wisdome to preuent his extremities.*

> . . . Base minded men, all three of you, if by my miserie you be not warnd: for vnto none of you (like mee) sought those burres to cleaue: those Puppets (I meane) that spake from our mouths, those Anticks garnisht in our colours. Is it not strange, that I, to whom they all haue beene beholding: is it not like that you, to whome they all haue beene beholding, shall (were yee in that case as I am now) bee both at once of them forsaken: Yes trust them not: for there is an vpstart Crow, beautified with our feathers, that with his *Tygers hart wrapt in a Players hyde,* supposes he is as well able to bom-

94

bast out a blanke verse as the best of you: and beeing an absolute *Iohannes fac totum,* is in his owne conceit the onely Shake-scene in a countrey. O that I might intreat your rare wits to be imploied in more profitable courses: & let those Apes imitate your past excellence, and neuer more acquaint them with your admired inuentions.

Greene liked to be somewhat cryptic, but to those in the know in the London theater world he made clear the identity of the actor-turned-playwright against whom he warned by his sneering phrase, "the onely Shake-scene in a countrey," coupled with the quotation from Act I, Scene 4 of *Henry VI, Part 3* of Shakespeare's line, "O tiger's heart wrapp'd in a woman's hide," which Greene parodies and makes appropriate to his attack by substituting "player's" for "woman's."

This first London reference to Shakespeare appropriately combines his acting and his writing functions, and the context of Greene's allusion makes it plain that Shakespeare's success as a playwright was already sufficient to make him a serious rival to the University Wits.

There was a sequel to Greene's bitter warnings. Since the manuscript was written on his death bed, Greene did not himself see it through the press and the office was performed for him by another prolific hand-to-mouth writer, Henry Chettle. Evidently there were repercussions from the passage Greene had addressed to the other University Wits, *"those Gentlemen his Quondam acquaintance,"* for his editor, Chettle, later said that the passage was "offensiuely by one or two of them taken." This comment Chettle made in the epistle to a pamphlet of his own entitled *Kind-Harts Dreame,* which was entered for publication just two and one-half months after Greene's pamphlet had been entered. He speaks of his part in getting Greene's pamphlet published and seeing it through the press, and refers cryptically to the two playwrights Greene had attacked or reproved, one of whom was probably Christopher Marlowe (whom Greene had previously begged to abandon the atheism they had once shared) and the other pretty certainly Shakespeare.

> About three moneths since died M. *Robert Greene,* leauing many papers in sundry Booke sellers hands, among other his Groatsworth of wit, in which a letter written to diuers play-makers, is offensiuely by one or two of them taken, and because on the dead they cannot be auenged, they wilfully . . . light on me . . . With neither of them that take offence was I acquainted, and with one of them I care not if I neuer be: The other, whome at that time I did not so much spare, as since I wish I had, for that as I haue moderated the heate of liuing writers, and might have vsde my owne discretion (especially in such a case) the Author beeing dead, that I did not, I am as sory, as if the originall fault had beene my fault, because my selfe haue seene his demeanor no lesse ciuill than he exelent in the qualitie he professes: Besides, diuers of worship haue reported his uprightnes of dealing, which argues his honesty, and his facetious grace in writting, that aprooues his Art. . . . I had onely in the copy this share, it was il written, as sometime *Greenes* hand was none of the best, licensd it must be, ere it could bee printed which could neuer be if it might not be read. To be briefe I writ it ouer, and as neare as I could, followed the copy, onely in that letter I put something out, but in the whole booke not a worde in, for I protest it was all *Greenes.* . . .

After one has untangled his syntax and his references, Henry Chettle seems to say that some time in the two and one-half months between the licensing of Greene's pamphlet on 20 September 1592 and the licensing of his own on 8 December he had heard of the objections to Greene's slighting words about Marlowe and Shakespeare. Though he was personally acquainted with neither playwright, since editing Greene's pamphlet he has seen Shakespeare's civil demeanor and observed his excellence in acting ("the qualitie he professes"). He has further heard men of good standing ("diuers of worship," not Bohemians like Robert Greene) report Shakespeare's upright dealings, and he has himself now observed his polished and urbane writing ("facetious grace"). Since nothing of Shakespeare's had been published before 8 December 1592, Chettle must either have seen manuscripts of Shakespeare's work or, more probably, attended a performance of one of his plays.

In the three years after the comments on him by Robert Greene and Henry Chettle, Shakespeare must have risen fast in the London theater world and in the acting company to which he belonged, for when he appears again he is a principal sharer in the company which was then one of the two leading London troupes and which soon became the most distinguished and successful dramatic troupe ever known in the history of the theater in English-speaking countries.

At the time of Greene's attack and for over a year after, the London theatrical situation was chaotic. The most distinguished company was declining; the hostile Lord Mayor and Corporation tried to get all acting of plays in London suppressed; companies combined and separated; theaters were closed because of rioting; and, worst of all, during the last half of 1592 and most of 1593 London suffered a frightful epidemic of the bubonic plague. This terrifying disease gripped London periodically during the sixteenth and seventeenth centuries, and during the worst epidemics, like those of 1593, 1603, 1609, and 1625, many thousands died in the city, sometimes as much as 10 per cent of the population in a few months, so that mass burials had to be resorted to. In such times the population became panicky. Many fled from London, and those who remained feared to leave their houses. When the death rate from the plague was very high, the theaters were always closed by edict, and the companies then tried to make a living by touring, but often the officials in the provincial towns, having heard of the London plague, refused to receive them. In such direful times, most dramatic companies went bankrupt.

At the end of the catastrophic plague-closing of 1592–93, two reorganized dramatic companies emerged as the principal, though not the only, London troupes. One was the Lord Admiral's company, financed by the theater magnate Philip Henslowe and headed by the great actor Edward Alleyn, and the other was the Lord Chamberlain's company, with an even greater actor, Richard Burbage, and a rising actor-playwright, William Shakespeare. For several years these two acting companies were the ranking ones, and they competed for distinction before the London theater audience and the court. By the end of Queen Elizabeth's reign the Lord Chamberlain's company was dominant and the obvious choice for the King's own company in the next reign. For forty years thereafter it knew no serious rival. This is the organization to which, after 1593, Shakespeare devoted most of his energies during his mature years. He never acted or wrote for any other troupe, and on his death bed, when his thoughts were mostly on his provisions for his family, he remembered his three principal colleagues of the Lord Chamberlain–King's company.

The next document in Shakespeare's acting career shows him as an official representative of this company. All London actors hoped for opportunities to perform before Queen Elizabeth at court. Not only were such command performances financially profitable, but the prestige accruing to the actors who at a single performance entertained the sovereign and a large part of the most distinguished figures of the time was unsurpassable. In his lifetime Shakespeare's company was so honored more often than all rival companies put together.

For a royal performance the play was selected and inspected by the Queen's Master of the Revels; a special stage was built at court; and the actors performed at night with candles and torches to illumine the scene and with much more splendor than they ordinarily achieved in their own theaters. Later, after their bill had been examined and certified, they were paid from the royal treasury, and two or three leading actors of the company signed the receipt for payment.

During the Christmas festivities of 1594, the Lord Chamberlain's company performed a play before Queen Elizabeth and her court on 26 December (St. Stephen's Day) and another on either 27 December (St. John's Day) or 28 December (Innocents' Day). The accounts say the 28th for the second play, but other records suggest that this is an error for the 27th. Two and one-half months later, when the bill for the two performances had been approved and the voucher sent through the government offices, leading sharers of the company signed a receipt for £20 for the performances, and the record of payment was entered in the official Declared Accounts now preserved in the Public Record Office in London. The record reads:

To Will[iam] Kempe Will[iam] Shakespeare &

Richarde Burbage seruantes to the Lord Chamb[er]leyne vpon the councelles warr[ant] dated at Whitehall xv^{to} Martii 1594 [1595 in the modern calendar] for twoe seuerall comedies or Enterludes shewed by them before her Ma[jesty] in [Christ]mas tyme laste paste viz vpon St Stephens daye & Innocentes daye xiij^l vj^s viij^d and by waye of her ma[jesty's] Rewarde vj^l xiij^s iiij^d in all xx^l

William Kempe was at this time the most popular comedian in London and a very valuable member of the company; Richard Burbage was well on the way to becoming the greatest English actor of the time and was a principal investor in the organization. The fact that Shakespeare signed for payment with these two men, the most valuable actors in the company, is a measure of his rapid advance in his profession and of his position of respect and responsibility in the Lord Chamberlain's company.

Another record of a different sort again attests Shakespeare's prominent position in his company. This record was made three years later by the most unconventional, as well as one of the most distinguished, of the Elizabethan and Jacobean playwrights, Ben Jonson. Perhaps his principal eccentricity was his conviction that his plays were a significant contribution to English literature and deserved therefore to be preserved for posterity, along with certain facts about their production. Such an attitude in a prominent playwright is conventional in the twentieth century, but Ben Jonson was the only dramatist of his time who thought so highly of his plays that he prepared them for posterity with revised texts, dramatis personae, dates of production, and sometimes even casts. Other dramatists gave little or no care to the preparation of their plays for the printers, and Shakespeare did not even take steps to see that his plays got printed, much less to provide dramatis personae or other conveniences for the reader.

This eccentricity of Jonson's led him at the age of about forty to collect his own plays, masques, and poems and to bring them out in a scrupulously edited volume that he entitled *The Workes of Ben Jonson*—occasioning the derision of many of his contemporaries. He printed first in this volume the play he thought to be his earliest important one, *Every Man in His Humour*. He noted when and by whom it was produced, and for the first time in English publishing he recorded the names of the actors who had created the roles. An indication of the unusual nature of this recognition of the actors is to be seen in the fact that in the hundreds of plays outside Jonson's that were published in London before the closing of the theaters there are only about a dozen printed casts. In the collection of 1616, the Jonson Folio, the author had printed at the end of *Every Man in His Humour,*

This Comœdie was first Acted, in the yeere 1598.

By the then L. Chamberlayne *his Seruants.*

The principall Comœdians were,

Will. Shakespeare.	Ric. Bvrbadge.
Avg. Philips.	Joh. Hemings.
Hen. Condel.	Tho. Pope.
Will. Slye.	Chr. Beeston.
Will. Kempe.	Joh. Dvke.

Though Jonson does not give the roles taken by the actors, the placing of Shakespeare high in the list indicates his prominence in the company.

Near the end of the year of the premiere of *Every Man in His Humour,* the leading sharers of the Lord

Chamberlain's company, including Shakespeare, took the first steps toward the erection of a new theater for the troupe. At that time there were already five or six public and private theaters in London, as well as several carrier inns, like the Cross Keys, the Bull, and the Bel Savage, which were often used for the performance of plays. In none of these theaters, however, did the actors themselves own a controlling interest; they paid rent to an owner whose interests were often in conflict with theirs, as they often are in modern dramatic enterprises.

In 1598 six of the leading actors of the Lord Chamberlain's company, together with the brother of one of them, began to make arrangements for a new theater to be called the Globe. First they leased from Nicholas Brend a plot of land across the Thames on the Bankside, not far from two existing theaters, the Rose and the Swan. The most direct statement about their actions was recorded some twenty years later in a document in a law suit preserved in the Public Record Office in London, in which two of Shakespeare's fellows, joint owners of the Globe, in reply to a claim for shares in the theater, recall for the court the origins of the enterprise:

> The ioynt and seuerall answers of John Hemings and Henry Condell gentlemen def[endants] to the bill of Complaint of John Witter gentleman Complaynant.

> The said Def[endants] . . . do say . . . the said gardens and groundes wherevpon the said Playhowse & galleryes were afterwardes builded were demised & letten by the said Nicholas Brend by his Jndenture of lease tripartite bearing date in or about the xxjth day of ffebruary in the xljth yeere of the raigne of the late Queene Elizabeth [1599 by mod-

ern calendar] vnto Cuthbert Burbadge Richard Burbadge William Shakespeare the said Augustine Phillipps Thomas Pope the said John Heminges one of the said def[endants], and William Kempe . . . from the ffeast of the birth of our Lord God Last past [i.e. 25 December 1598] before the date of the said Jndenture vnto thend & terme of xxxj yeeres from thence next ensuing for the yeerely rent of seaven poundes & five shillinges. . . . Which said W[illiam] Shakespeare Augustine Phillipps Thomas Pope John Heminges & William Kempe did shortlie after graunte & assigne all the said Moitie of & in the said gardens & groundes vnto William Levison and Thomas Savage, who re-graunted & reassigned to euerye of them seuerally a fift parte of the said Moitie of the said garden & groundes, Vpon w[hich] premisses or some parte thereof there was shortly after built the said then playhowse. So as the said Augustine Phillipps had a fiveth parte of the moitie of the said gardens & groundes & after the said Playhowse was built he had a fiveth parte of the said galleryes of the said Playhowse, in ioynt tenancie with the said William Shakespeare Thomas Pope the said John Heminges & W[illiam] Kempe. . . .

This statement indicates that the actors had come to an agreement to lease the land of Nicholas Brend before Christmas, 1598, the date of the beginning of the term of the lease. The assignments and reassignments are devices to give half the ownership of the new Globe to Cuthbert and Richard Burbage, whose father had bequeathed them The Theatre (from whose timbers the Globe was built), and to divide the other half equally among Shakespeare, Phillipps, Pope, Heminges, and Kempe. In other words, Shakespeare owned 10 per cent, and Cuthbert and Richard Burbage each owned 25 per cent of the new theater. Six of the seven men involved were leading sharers of the Lord Chamberlain's company whom Jonson had listed as performers in the same year, 1598, at the opening of *Every Man in His Humour*. Thus Shakespeare was not only a sharer, or patented member, of the Lord Chamberlain's company, but after the building of the Globe in 1599 he was a part owner, or housekeeper, as well.

The new playhouse was erected from the timbers of its demolished predecessor, The Theatre, as is indicated in another suit preserved in the Public Record Office that was brought against the Burbages in 1601 for their razing of the building. The plaintiff in this suit, Giles Alleyn, who had leased to the Burbages' father the ground on which The Theatre had been built, and who was much annoyed by the Burbages' successful removal of their property, recounts the action in his complaint:

> . . . the sayd Cuthbert Burbage . . . wth the sayd Richard Burbage and one Peeter Streat, William Smyth and diuers other persons to the number of twelve to your Subiect vnknowne did aboute the eight and twentyth daye of December in the one and fortyth yeere of your highnes Raygne [i.e. 1598] . . . ryotouslye assemble themselves together and then and there armed themselves wth divers and manye vnlawfull and offensive weapons, as namelye swordes daggers billes axes and such like And soe armed did then repayre vnto the sayd Theater And then and there armed as aforesayd in a verye ryotous outragious and forcyble manner and contrarye to the lawes of your highnes Realme attempted to pull downe the sayd Theater . . . And having so done did then also in most forcible and ryotous manner take and carrye awaye from thence

all the wood and timber therof vnto the Banckside
in the parishe of St Marye Overyes and there erected a newe playe howse wth the sayd Timber and
wood.

Whether Shakespeare himself was present at this interesting demolition of The Theatre no one knows,
but certainly he was very much concerned, for the lease
of the ground for the Globe had already begun its term
three days before. Shakespeare was a party to this lease,
and he and his fellows needed The Theatre timbers in
order to begin construction on their new Bankside playhouse.

The violent terms in which Giles Alleyn describes
the pulling down of The Theatre were obviously designed to prejudice the court against the Burbages, for
their lease from Alleyn (still extant) explicitly gave
them the right to tear down their playhouse and re-
move the materials.

How soon the Burbages and Shakespeare and their
fellows were able to put on plays at the Globe is unknown, but it must have been soon, for when an inventory of the property of Thomas Brend, father of
Nicholas, was made about 16 May 1599, one item listed
was

> . . . vna domo de novo edificata . . . in parochia
> Sci Salvatoris praedicta in comitatu Surria prae-
> dicta in occupacione Willielmi Shakespeare et ali-
> orum. [a house newly built in the parish of St.
> Saviour aforesaid in the county of Surrey afore-
> said in the occupation of William Shakespeare and
> others]

The "St Marye Overyes" of Alleyn's complaint and
"Sci Salvatoris" or St. Saviour's in Nicholas Brend's inventory are simply the medieval and the renaissance

names for the same parish; St. Saviour's is the name used now, but both were used in the late sixteenth and early seventeenth centuries.

In the new Globe in the parish of St. Saviour's Southwark, the Lord Chamberlain's men settled in for a long and prosperous career. Part of their success was due to the plays written for the house by one of the fellows of the company, William Shakespeare; part was due to the drawing power of the greatest actor of his time, another fellow of the company, Richard Burbage; and part was due to the unique organization of the enterprise by which several of the fellows of the company were not only actors but owners of the company's theater as well, so that nearly all the profits from the actors' work stayed with the actors themselves. The development of this arrangement, of which Shakespeare as one of the actor-owners was long a part, is outlined in another legal document drafted about twenty years after the dramatist's death. In 1635 certain of the members of Shakespeare's company, which was still prominent and still acting his plays, were trying to get the ownership of shares in the company's two theaters still more widely distributed among the actors. In reply to their petition the surviving Burbages—Richard's brother Cuthbert, his wife Winifred, and his son William—recount London theatrical history leading up to the Globe enterprise.

The father of vs Cutbert & Rich[ard] Burbage was the first builder of Playhowses & was himselfe in his younger yeeres a Player. The Theater hee built w[ith] many Hundred poundes taken vp at interest. The Players that liued in those first times had onely the profitts arising from the dores, but now the players receaue all the commings in at the dores to them selues & halfe the Galleries from the

Houskeepers. Hee [i.e. James Burbage, father of Cuthbert and Richard] built this house vpon leased ground, by w[hich] meanes the Landlord [i.e. Giles Alleyn] & Hee had a great suite in law & by his death, the like troubles fell on vs, his sonnes; wee then bethought vs of altering from thence, & at like expence built the Globe w[ith] more summes of money taken vp at interest, which lay heauy on vs many yeeres, & to o[ur] selues wee ioyned those deseruing men, Shakspere Hemings, Condall, Philips and others partners in [the] profittes of that they call the House.

Two or three years after the Lord Chamberlain's company began performing in their new Bankside theater called the Globe, a London law student set down in his diary an anecdote about two of the leading sharers in the troupe. This young man, John Manningham, used his diary as a commonplace book to record stories, current events, poems, epigrams, anecdotes, proverbs, sermon notes, prescriptions, and other trivia that seemed important at the time and that he thought he would like to remember. He noted, for instance, the current gossip about such figures as Queen Elizabeth, Sir Walter Raleigh, John Marston, Ben Jonson, and Sir Thomas Bodley, and often he added a name at the end of the anecdote so that he could remember who had told him the story.

On 13 March 1601 (1602 in the modern calendar), he wrote down a tale about the greatest actor of the day in a role that his fellow Shakespeare had written for him in one of his best-known plays, a piece composed several years before but still popular in the theater and on the book stalls. The anecdote neatly, if scandalously, couples two of the leading members of the company at the Globe. Manningham wrote,

Vpon a tyme when Burbidge played Rich. 3: there
was a Citizen greue soe farr in liking wth him, that
before shee went from the play shee appointed him
to come that night vnto hir by the name of Ri:/
the 3./// Shakespeare ouerhearing their conclu-
sion, went before, was intertained, and at his game
ere Burbidge came /// Then message being
brought that Rich. the 3^d. was at the dore Shakespeare caused returne to be made that William the
Conquerour was before Rich. the 3 /// Shakespeares name Wllm   Mr Curle:/

Whatever the truth of the anecdote that young John
Manningham heard from his roommate Edward Curle,
it displays an obvious familiarity with the association of
the two actors Burbage and Shakespeare at the Globe.

The same Burbage-Shakespeare association was also
familiar to undergraduates of the time at Cambridge
University. At certain colleges of Oxford and Cambridge, plays were frequently performed by students
on festive occasions. Some of them were Latin plays by
ancient and medieval authors; many were new plays
written in Latin by students or by Fellows of the colleges, but quite a few were contemporary plays written
in English by the undergraduates. Among the best-
known of these last is a series of three plays presented
in the Christmas season by the undergraduates of St.
John's College, Cambridge, in three different years at
the turn of the century. They were called *The Pilgrimage to Parnassus, The First Part of the Returne from
Parnassus,* and *The Second Part of the Returne from
Parnassus;* the first one, *The Pilgrimage,* deals with
undergraduate life at Cambridge, and the second and
third with the troubles of new graduates. *The Second
Part of the Returne from Parnassus,* the last of the
three plays, was prepared for performance by the stu-

dents of St. John's College probably in early January 1602 (modern calendar). It is a satiric play in which the troubles of the university men who find little respect for their learning in the cold world are variously presented. Most of the characters are recent graduates of Cambridge who are struggling to make a living, but in the fourth act two new characters appear, Shakespeare's fellows Richard Burbage and Will Kempe, the same two who had been recipients with Shakespeare of the company's fees for court performances seven years before. The poor graduates, Studioso and Philomusus, are to have try-outs with Burbage and Kempe to see if they can be hired as actors for the Lord Chamberlain's company. Before the graduates come on, Burbage and Kempe discuss their possible usefulness to the company. Kempe objects to the acting of University players.

BURBAGE. A little teaching will mend these faults, and it may bee besides they will be able to pen a part.

KEMPE. Few of the vniuersity [men] pen plaies well, they smell too much of that writer *Ouid,* and that writer *Metamorphoses,* and talke too much of *Proserpina* & *Iuppiter.* Why heres our fellow *Shakespeare* puts them all downe, I and *Ben Ionson* too. O that *Ben Ionson* is a pestilent fellow, he brought vp *Horace* giuing the Poets a pill, but our fellow *Shakespeare* hath giuen him a purge that made him beray his credit.

Then the student candidates come on, and Kempe tells them how good it is to be an actor:

be merry my lads, you haue happened vpon the most excellent vocation in the world: for money, they come North and South to bring it to our play-house, and for honour, who of more report than

Dick Burbage & *Will Kempe?* Hee's not counted a Gentleman that knows not *Dick Burbage* & *Wil Kemp,* there's not a country wench that can dance Sellengers Round but can talke of *Dick Burbage* and *Will. Kempe.*

The two aspiring graduates then have their try-outs, the first reading a famous passage from Thomas Kyd's *Spanish Tragedy,* and the second repeating after Kempe a comic passage from an unknown play. Then Richard Burbage seems to see tragic possibilities in Philomusus and says:

I like your face and the proportion of your body for *Richard* the 3. I pray [you] M. *Philomusus* let me see you act a little of it.

PHILOMUSUS. Now is the winter of our discontent Made glorious summer by the sonne of Yorke, [&c.]

BURBAGE. Very well I assure you. Well M. *Philomusus* and M. *Studioso,* wee see what ability you are of: I pray walke with vs to our fellows, and weele agree presently.

In the tone of these lines one may see a suggestion of the attitude of the University Wits toward the players and their actor-dramatist which had been revealed in a more virulent form nearly ten years before by Robert Greene in his *Groats-worth of Wit.* But the Cambridge students, whatever their critical judgment of successful actors, current writing, and classic masterpieces, show a confident knowledge of Shakespeare in the context of the Fellows of his company. The selection as the try-out passage for Philomusus of the familiar opening of one of Shakespeare's most popular plays, in which Burbage himself was famous, again illustrates current knowledge of William Shakespeare as the actor-dramatist of the Lord Chamberlain's company and a fellow of Burbage and Kempe.

A little more than a year after the Cambridge performance, Queen Elizabeth died and King James of Scotland came down to England as her successor. In the new reign the Lord Chamberlain's company as the most distinguished in the realm became the King's troupe, while the other regular London acting companies took the names of less exalted members of the royal family: Queen Anne's company, Prince Henry's company.

As royal players, Shakespeare and his fellows attained a new status and a new patent, and, as other documents show, they were entitled to wear royal livery. Ten days after King James's arrival in London the royal secretary sent the King's order or warrant to Lord Cecil, the Keeper of the Privy Seal, to prepare for the company letters patent under the great seal of England. This warrant is still extant in the Public Record Office in London.

By the king

Right trusty and welbeloued Counsello^r we greete you well and will and Commannd you y^t vnder our priuie Seale in yor Custody for the time being you Cause o^r l[ette]rs to be directed to the keep[er] of o^r greate seale of England Commannding him y^t vnder o^r said greate Seale he cause o^r l[ett]res to be made patentes in forme following. James by the grace of God king of England . . . To all Iustices Maiors Sheriffes Constables Hedboroughes . . . Know ye y^t we of o^r speciall grace . . . have licenced and authorized . . . these o^r seruantes Lawrence ffletcher, William Shakespeare Richard Burbage Augustine Phillippes John Heminges Henry Condell William Sly Robt Armyn Richard

Cowlye and the rest of their associates freely to vse
and exercise the Arte and facultie of playing Comedies Tragedies Histories Enterludes Moralles Pas-
toralles Stage plaies & such other like as they haue
already studied or heerafter shall vse or studie . . .
w^{th}in theire now vsuall howse called the Globe . . .
Giuen vnder o^r Signet at our Manno^r of Green-
wiche the seavententh day of May in the first yeere
of o^r raigne of England ffraunce and Irland, and of
Scotland the six and thirtieth [1603].

From this warrant, and following its wording, the
royal patent for the King's company was prepared. It
has been quoted above (pp. 91–92) as an example of patents for players. As the King's own company, Shakespeare and his fellows at the Globe had no serious
rivals in the kingdom.

In the year of their new royal patent Shakespeare is
again recorded as the creator of one of the roles in a
Ben Jonson play. The tragedy called *Sejanus His Fall,*
though not popular on its first presentation, became
one of the three or four most famous tragedies of the
reign. When Jonson collected his plays for publication
in 1616 he had this one printed with the statement:

This Tragœdie was first acted, in the yeere 1603.
By the Kings Maiesties Seruants. The principall
Tragœdians were,

Ric. Bvrbadge.	Will. Shake-Speare.
Avg. Philips.	Ioh. Hemings.
Will. Sly.	Hen. Condel.
Ioh. Lowin.	Alex. Cooke.

The new status of Shakespeare and his fellow actors
as the King's players gave them occasional privileges
and duties which were not histrionic. One was the receipt of special livery on the occasion of the royal pro-

cession when London celebrated the accession of the new king. When King James first came down from Scotland, London was suffering another epidemic of bubonic plague and all public gatherings were curtailed. It was nearly a year before the city was recovered enough to celebrate, and then a great procession through triumphal arches and past symbolic tableaux was arranged for 15 March 1604 (modern calendar). On this occasion the King's players, like many other attendants in the royal establishment, were made special allowances for new liveries for the procession, as recorded in the accounts of Sir George Home, Master of the Great Wardrobe:

	Red cloth
William Shakespeare	iiij yardes di.
Augustine Phillipps	"
Lawrence Fletcher	"
John Hemminges	"
Richard Burbidge	"
William Slye	"
Robert Armyn	"
Henry Cundell	"
Richard Cowley	"

Later in the same year special attendance of the King's men was required at Somerset House (the Queen's palace), where the new Spanish Ambassador and his train were being entertained during peace negotiations. The nature of the attendance of the players is not known, nor is Shakespeare mentioned by name, but he was, of course, one of the "ffellowes" of Phillipps and Hemings who were paid for attendance, according to the account preserved in the records of the Audit Office.

To Augustine Phillippes and John Hemynges for thallowaunce of themselves and tenne of theire ffellowes his ma^{tes} groomes of the chamber, and Players for waytinge and attendinge on his ma^{tes} service by commaundemente vppon the Spanishe Embassador at Som[er]sette howse the space of xviij dayes viz^d from the ixth day of Auguste 1604 vntill the xxvijth day of the same as appeareth by a bill thereof signed by the Lord Chamb[er]layne xxj^{li}. xij^s.

Augustine Phillipps, who is here joint payee with John Heminges for the company and who had been a fellow of Shakespeare for ten years, died a few months after he collected this fee for the attendance of his fellows on the Spanish Ambassador. When he made his will on 4 May 1605 he had his companions in the King's company very much in mind and remembered players of all ranks in the company, distinguishing carefully among fellows, hired men, and boys or apprentices in his bequests:

Item I geve and bequeathe unto and amongste the hyred men of the Company which I am of . . . the some of fyve pounds . . . to be equally distributed amongeste them, Item I geve and bequeathe to my Fellowe William Shakespeare a thirty shillings peece in gould, To my Fellowe Henry Condell one other thirty shillinge peece in gould, To my Servaunte Christopher Beeston thirty shillings in gould, To my Fellowe Lawrence Fletcher twenty shillings in gould, To my Fellowe Robert Armyne twenty shillings in gould, To my fellowe Richard Coweley twenty shillings in gould, To my fellowe Alexander Cook twenty shillings in gould, To my fellowe Nicholas Tooley twenty shillings in gould . . . Item, I geve to Samuell Gilborne my late apprentice, the some of fortye shillings, and my mouse colloured velvit hose, and a white taffety

114

dublet, a blacke taffety sute, my purple cloke, sword and dagger, and my base viall. Item I geve to James Sands my Apprentice the some of fortye shillings and a citterne a bandore and a lute, to be paid and delivered unto him at the expiracion of his terme of yeres in his indenture of apprentice-hood.

The respect and affection among the members of the King's company implied by the bequests in this will may give an indication of the environment in which Shakespeare was writing and acting at the Globe.

That theater, since its completion in 1599, had been the London playhouse of the Lord Chamberlain–King's company; its stage was what Shakespeare had in mind when he wrote most of his greatest plays. No other company ever acted at the Globe, and in the mind of Londoners the Globe Theatre and the King's men were identified. Then in 1608 the company acquired a second theater, the Blackfriars. Whereas the Globe was a large public theater where general admission was cheap and where the groundlings in the pit stood exposed to sun and rain, the Blackfriars was a private theater. It was small, exclusive because there were no cheap admissions, completely sheltered from the weather, and planned for candlelight, not daylight performances. It had been made some years before in 1596 by remodeling certain rooms in the old Dominican priory, about one hundred yards southwest of St. Paul's Cathedral. The builder was James Burbage, father of Richard and Cuthbert, who had built The Theatre twenty years before.

From 1596 to 1608 Blackfriars had been leased, like all the other private theaters, to boy companies who catered to rather exclusive audiences. Then in 1608 Richard and Cuthbert, who had inherited the Blackfriars at the death of their father, arranged with certain of the patented members of the King's company to provide the Blackfriars as a second theater for the King's men. Years later the surviving Burbages in a suit brought in 1635 recalled the early history of Blackfriars.

> Now for the Blackfriers that is o[r] inheritance, o[r] father purchased it at extreame rates & made it into a play house wth great charge & trouble, which after was leased out to one Euans that first sett vp the Boyes commonly called the Queenes Ma[jesty's] Children of the Chappell. In processe of time the boyes growing vp to bee men which were Vnderwood, Field, Ostler, & were taken to strengthen the Kings service, & the more to strengthen the service, the boyes dayly wearing out, it was considered that house would bee as fitt for o[r] selues, & soe purchased the lease remaining from Evans wth o[r] money & placed men Players, which were Hemings, Condall Shakespeare &c.

What the Burbages did when they transferred the Blackfriars to the use of the King's men is set out in an earlier suit about the ownership of shares in the playhouse. They formed a group of seven men consisting of Richard Burbage, Cuthbert Burbage, Thomas Evans, William Shakespeare, John Heminges, Henry Condell, and William Slye, who on 9 August 1608 leased the Blackfriars for a period of twenty-one years at an annual rental of £40, of which sum each man was responsible for one-seventh, or £5 14s. 4d. These provisions are learned indirectly from a suit which Thomasine Ostler brought in 1615 to force John Heminges to pay her returns from shares held by her deceased husband, William Ostler.

Five of the seven men who leased the Blackfriars theater were also fellows of the King's company, so that in the Blackfriars as in the Globe the "housekeepers," to whom the actors paid a portion of their receipts as rent, were also actors, and the profits of the dramatic enterprise continued to stay almost entirely in the hands of the acting group. Thus for more than half of his career in London Shakespeare shared in the enterprise of the Lord Chamberlain–King's company as actor, patented member, dramatist, and housekeeper, first of the Globe and then of both the Globe and Blackfriars. No other man of the time is known to have been tied to the theater in so many different ways.

These Blackfriars records are the last that show Shakespeare as actor, sharer, and housekeeper in London. By 1612, though he continued to prepare plays for his company, he had apparently retired to Stratford, for, as we have seen, when he testified for Stephen Belott in the Belott-Mountjoy suit in May 1612, he identified himself as of Stratford-upon-Avon (see above, pp. 79–80).

His company, however, continued to think of Shakespeare as an actor and their fellow. Several years after his death, the two oldest sharers in the King's company, who had been colleagues of Shakespeare for twenty years or more, gathered his plays together for a collected volume. In the dedication they speak of their purpose as

> onely to keepe the memory of so worthy a Friend, & Fellow aliue, as was our *Shakespeare*.

And they prepared for this edition an unusual piece of front matter which emphasizes that the plays are vehicles for actors and names Shakespeare himself as the first actor. The last item before the Table of Plays in the First Folio is:

The Names of the Principall Actors in all
these Playes.

William Shakespeare.   Samuel Gilburne.
Richard Burbadge.   Robert Armin.
John Hemmings.   William Ostler.
Augustine Phillips.   Nathan Field.
William Kempt.   John Vnderwood.
Thomas Poope.   Nicholas Tooley.
George Bryan.   William Ecclestone.
Henry Condell.   Joseph Taylor.
William Slye.   Robert Benfield.
Richard Cowly.   Robert Goughe.
John Lowine.   Richard Robinson.
Samuell Crosse.   Iohn Shancke.
Alexander Cooke.   Iohn Rice.

CHAPTER 5

The Playwright

W E have seen that the records preserved from the sixteenth and seventeenth centuries show William Shakespeare to have been a man of varied interests and activities. He acted in plays, he owned shares in and apparently helped to direct the leading dramatic company of the day, he owned shares in theaters, he bought and sold houses and land, he bought and sold grain, he wrote narrative poems and sonnets, and occasionally he served as an attendant of the King. These multiple activities are clearly shown in the documents which chance has preserved from his lifetime, but none of the records so far noticed exhibits his principal preoccupation. During his working years the great preponderance of his time and of his fabulous intellectual energy was devoted to the writing of plays. By profession Shakespeare was a man of the theater, and the most complete man of the theater of his time.

More than 300 English playwrights who wrote during the reigns of Elizabeth, James I, and Charles I are still known to us, and much information about their lives and activities has been collected. Many wrote a few occasional plays but devoted most of their time to other pursuits: they were amateur dramatists, like the physician Thomas Lodge, or the courtier and fiction writer John Lyly, or the pamphleteer and novelist Robert Greene, or the lawyer John Ford. Somewhat more fully concerned with the playhouses than these amateurs were the semiprofessionals who derived part of their living from the commercial theaters but rather more from noble or royal patrons, and who devoted much of their time to writing that was not intended for professional actors, men like George Chapman and Ben Jonson.

The completely professional playwrights were those who made their living by keeping the actors supplied with plays, writers who were wholly devoted to the theater: Thomas Heywood, James Shirley, William Rowley, Richard Brome, and William Shakespeare. Among these professionals a few were even more fully involved in theatrical affairs than the others, for they not only wrote plays but acted in them: the actor-dramatists Thomas Heywood, William Rowley, Nathan Field, and William Shakespeare. More completely than the other professional playwrights, these actor-dramatists were men of the theater, for they not only prepared their plays in close cooperation with the actors, as the other professionals did, but were themselves part of the troupe which tried out in the theater the effects that they, as playwrights, had prepared for the stage.

As one of this group of actor-dramatists Shakespeare was more "theater-tainted" than other famous Elizabethan dramatists, Thomas Kyd, Christopher Marlowe, John Lyly, Ben Jonson, George Chapman, John Webster, John Fletcher, and James Shirley. Actually he was more completely a man of the theater than even the other actor-dramatists, for as we have seen, he was associated with still another aspect of "show business": among the 300 and more authors who contributed to the great achievement commonly called the Elizabethan drama, he is the only one who is known to have been, over a long period of years, a theater owner.

Thus to say that Shakespeare, in spite of his various nondramatic activities, was the most complete man of the theater in his time is only to summarize the comprehensiveness of his participation in all aspects of the theatrical enterprise, as professional playwright, as actor, as "sharer," and as theater owner. The theater was clearly his chosen environment, and when we direct our attention to Shakespeare the playwright, we have come to the essential man.

In the writing of plays, as in the writing of biographies, Elizabethan customs were unlike the modern ones we take for granted. The most significant differences lie in the relationship between the dramatist and the company of actors who eventually performed his play. The modern dramatist usually begins with an idea or a situation or a story and does not concern himself much with cast or producer until he has completed a manuscript. When it is finished he is usually still not sure of his producer, and often his agent peddles the manuscript for some time before it is accepted and casting begins. Even after casting has started, neither author nor producer is entirely sure what actors he will get, and it sometimes happens that a role has to be altered because the producer cannot find an actor who can sing well enough, or is big enough or young enough for the role as originally written. When the modern dramatist writes another play, it never has the same cast as the first, often not the same producer, and very seldom the same theater.

None of these familiar modern conditions applied to Shakespeare or to his rival dramatists who produced plays for competing companies. Elizabethan playwrights of all kinds—amateurs like Lodge and Ford, semiprofessionals like Jonson and Chapman, professionals like Heywood and Shirley—ordinarily knew before they had gone very far with a manuscript what company, what particular actors, and what theater would produce the play when the manuscript was finished. The professional, and even a number of the semiprofessionals, knew before they set pen to paper all the characteristics of each actor for whom a main role was being written—whether the leading man would be tall or short, good at repartee or better at serious soliloquies, a fine dancer or a stately stalker, rather young or already past fifty, quiet and subtle or broad and energetic. They knew in advance whether the boy who was to play the leading female role could sing well, indifferently, or not at all, whether he was short or almost as tall as most of the men, whether he was best at the tomboy roles, the flirtatious roles, the modest and shy roles, or the limpid-eyed and suffering roles.

All dramatists in the period when Shakespeare was writing had this close knowledge of the men and boys who would act in their plays; Shakespeare differs from the rest only in the degree to which his familiarity extends. As actor, playwright, theater-owner, and sharer in a single company, he was involved in all phases of the activities of that company, with which he had, in the end, an unbroken experience of more than twenty years.

When Shakespeare wrote a play, then, he always began, unlike modern dramatists, with the company. What his fellows of the Lord Chamberlain–King's company could do, he asked them to do; what they could not do, he left out of the play, and the marks of these inclusions and exclusions are seen in everything he wrote for the theater.

To begin with the most obvious mark of these written-to-order plays, it is notable that Shakespeare always had in mind, as he wrote, the size of his producing company. Whereas a modern dramatist may vary the number in his cast from two or three (in plays like *Two for the See-Saw* or *The Voice of the Turtle*) to fifty or sixty (in *The Green Pastures* and *My Fair Lady*)—relying on the producer to hire the number of actors needed— Shakespeare always had to take into account the number of sharers, hired men, and boys in his own company. Though this number increased from the early days of the company until 1613 or 1614 when Shakespeare's last plays were written, the records of the company show that he must always have had available sixteen performers, including stage-keepers, box-holders, and musicians who could be pressed into service for crowd scenes or short bits in the plays, and that even in the later days he could probably never count on more than twenty-five. He clearly tried to use all the regulars in nearly all the plays, and since, so far as we know, extras were never hired, he never created parts not fitted to the actors of his own troupe.

This basic condition of the Elizabethan playwright's method of composition is displayed in the dramatis personae of every play that Shakespeare wrote. No plays with dramatis personae as small as three or four, or even as small as eight or nine—sizes common enough in modern plays—are found in the Shakespeare canon. All the actors of the Lord Chamberlain–King's company were always on the payroll, and as a faithful sharer in the company Shakespeare uses all of them, or nearly all of them, in every play. Always there are fifteen or more parts, though some may be small. In the history plays as many as forty or fifty characters appear, but the number of actors required has not been increased: Shakespeare has carefully arranged the play so that roles may be doubled and one actor may take two or even three parts. The prompt manuscript of

Believe as You List, a play written by Philip Massinger for the company after Shakespeare's death, still exists and demonstrates how the doubling was done. The play has about forty-eight roles, counting walk-ons like Roman soldiers. Though the King's company was larger when this play was prepared in 1631, several of Shakespeare's fellows were still acting, and the same methods of doubling prevailed. The casting in this prompt book has not been completed, but it clearly shows that twenty-eight of the forty-eight roles were acted by eighteen players. The manuscript does not indicate the performers for the other nineteen roles, mostly minor ones, but at least eight other actors who are not named in the manuscript were available to the company in 1631.

Thirty-two years before the prompter of the King's company prepared the manuscript of *Believe as You List,* a foreign visitor to London saw a performance of one of Shakespeare's plays, and his account of the experience suggests how Shakespeare at that time, when the company was much smaller, planned his plays to fit the size of the troupe. The visitor was Thomas Platter from Basle, who was in London during the autumn of 1599 and saw various of the sights. On the afternoon of the twenty-first of September 1599, he crossed the Thames from the city to the Bankside to attend a performance of *Julius Caesar* at the Globe. In his German account of his travels, Platter wrote of this experience:

> After lunch on 21 September, round about 2 o'-clock, I went with my companions across the water, and in the straw-thatched house saw the tragedy of the first emperor, Julius Caesar, excellently performed by some fifteen persons.

Since there are about forty speaking parts in *Julius Caesar,* Shakespeare in 1599 was arranging his plays for more extensive doubling than Philip Massinger had to allow for in 1631 when the company had grown to more than twice its former size.

The practice of preparing plays for doubling was ancient and standard in the Elizabethan theater. More than a dozen of the plays published in the twenty-five years before Shakespeare came to London even show in title-page charts how judicious doubling will enable the play to be performed with about one-third as many actors as there are roles. For example, about the time that *King Lear* was performed, Thomas Heywood's *Fair Maid of the Exchange* was published with the dramatis personae arranged to show how the twenty-one parts could be handled by eleven actors. Shakespeare simply followed a well-known method of play-writing in planning *Henry VIII* (which was being acted with such splendor at the Globe in 1613 when the theater burned down during a performance) so that its forty-one speaking parts required only about the same number of actors as *Othello* with thirteen. Always Shakespeare designed the play not for an ideal company but for the peculiarities of his own company at the time in which he was writing.

Another obvious influence of the personnel of the Lord Chamberlain–King's company on his plays is to be seen in Shakespeare's handling of female roles. Females were not permitted to act on the Elizabethan stage, and boys with unchanged voices had therefore to be used. The number of boys to choose from in the company was always small, and the very fact of their youth made it impossible that they could be as experienced actors as the men. Moreover, the boys literally outgrew their roles—as the Burbages phrased it in their account of the company's acquisition of the Blackfriars theater, "the boyes dayly wearing out." New children had constantly to be recruited, and at any given time, therefore, several of the boys in the troupe would be too new and too inexperienced to handle sustained or difficult roles; though they could do small parts like the ladies at the ball in *Romeo and Juliet,* or the ladies of the court in the second act of *Hamlet,* they would not be up to major parts. Mindful of this situation in his company, Shakespeare created comparatively few female roles. In most of the plays there are only two to four women important enough to be given names, while there are ten to twenty named parts for men. In some of the histories, *Henry IV, Part 2,* for example, there are as many as thirty-five named parts for men but only four for women, and even these did not require four different boy actors, for two of the women appear in one scene only, and the same two boys could easily be used for all four women's parts.

The limitations of the boy actors affected the playwright in numerous other ways. He could not create women's parts which show much development of character—in *King Lear,* for instance, while Lear, Gloucester, Edgar, Edmund, Kent, and the Fool are all subtly developed characters, Cordelia, the most important of the women in the play and one of Shakespeare's major creations, has fewer lines than a minor character like the Duke of Albany. Shakespeare could not, as a rule, entrust the leading role to a boy actor: though he wrote all or parts of thirty-eight plays, he made a woman's part the largest in only four of them—Rosalind in *As You Like It,* Imogen in *Cymbeline,* Portia in *The Merchant of Venice,* and Helena in *All's Well That Ends Well.* At once others of Shakespeare's brilliant female characters spring to mind—Lady Macbeth, Cleopatra, Juliet, Viola—but they do not by any means have the longest roles in their plays.

Another instance of the restrictions that the nature of the company placed on the dramatist is to be seen in the character of the female roles in Shakespeare's plays. Though one can say that almost all kinds of men are to be found in his plays, one could never say that all kinds of women are there. Certain limited types are repeated again and again with subtle variations, while many other kinds of women who appear in the poetry and fiction of the time and whose real-life counterparts certainly lived in London are scarcely to be found in the plays at all.

The feminine role most frequently repeated is that of the young woman in love who is either gay and flirtatious or rather grave and sentimental. The first is most familiar in Rosalind, Nerissa, Beatrice, and Ann Page, roles which were well within the range of a clever boy actor. The second type, the serious, often touching and wistful young woman, is usually in an unfortunate situation and rouses sentimental concern or sometimes pity: Celia, Hero, Olivia, Desdemona, Ophelia, Perdita, Miranda, Cordelia, and Imogen. Again the role is within the capacity of a boy actor who has been carefully and strenuously trained.

It is interesting to observe what Shakespeare does *not* ask his boys to do. For instance, though they could be flirtatious or grave, gay or despondent, it would have been extremely difficult for them to carry off a sustained maternal role. This is the reason that while many of Shakespeare's heroines appear in the plays with their fathers, they seldom appear with their mothers. Cordelia, Desdemona, Imogen, Perdita, Ophelia, Jessica, Miranda, and Kate of *The Taming of the Shrew* all are shown with their fathers, but the mothers in all these plays are dead. Shakespeare avoided perfectly normal human situations if they demanded too much of his boy actors.

For the same reason, when the dramatist does include a mother with her child in a play he either makes the mother's part a very small one, like that of Lady Mac-duff, or else he carefully avoids situations in which a display of normal maternal love is required. Note the scenes in which Lady Capulet appears with her daughter Juliet, scenes in which the mother is giving her daughter formal advice, berating her, or mourning her supposed death. Or the formal and unemotional scenes of Mistress Page with her daughter Ann. Or even more striking, the scenes of Volumnia with her son Corio-lanus, in which she lectures him like a general on his duty to go out and get wounded for Rome. In the most famous mother–son relationship in all his plays, Queen Gertrude is given little chance to display normal maternal love for Hamlet. Shakespeare allows her to appear with Hamlet chiefly in public with all the court about her, and in her private scene with him, Hamlet berates her for her sins—scarcely a normal mother–son relationship. No more normal is that in *Richard III,* where the old Duchess of York appears with her son Richard mostly to curse him as a sinful monster.

Obviously Shakespeare's dramatic presentation of women is by no means a complete transcript of what he saw about him in London and Stratford, nor is it any indication that he disbelieved in mother love, or that he disliked women. He was writing for the London stage, not striving to present a rounded picture of Elizabethan life for posterity. He limited the number of female roles in his plays, he reduced their length, and he restricted their character, all because of the requirements of the Lord Chamberlain–King's company.

In the preparation of roles for the men of his company, Shakespeare was equally careful to exploit the talents that the company had, to avoid writing into any role requirements that would expose the weaknesses of the intended actor, and to take advantage of special talents. Characters in Shakespeare's plays sing not simply because a song would be effective in building the required mood of the scene but because the actor for whom the role was planned was a singer. The roles for the principal comedian in the plays written before 1599 are quite different from the comedian's roles in the plays written later because before 1599 one of the principal sharers of the company was a famous comedian named William Kempe whose farcical tricks, clownish bumbling, and dancing were widely enjoyed and frequently mentioned in print. Kempe was particularly famous as a dancer; he once danced all the way from London to Norwich, a distance of over 100 miles, and his buskins were hung up in the Guildhall at Norwich, where they became one of the sights for visitors. On his return Kempe published a pamphlet about his feat which he entitled *Kemp's Nine Days' Wonder*. With such a popular comedian in his troupe, Shakespeare created comic roles that would allow Kempe to display to the public the drollery and bumbling for which he was famous, roles like Costard in *Love's Labour's Lost,* Launce in *The Two Gentlemen of Verona,* Bottom in *A Midsummer Night's Dream,* and Dogberry in *Much Ado about Nothing.* When Kempe was succeeded as principal comic of the company by an experienced actor named Robert Armin who was the melancholy type of singing comedian, the old bumbling clown character disappears from the plays, and we find more subtle comic roles, like Feste in *Twelfth Night,* the First Grave-digger in *Hamlet,* and the Fool in *King Lear.*

Just as Shakespeare, the complete man of the theater, planned his plays so that they would avoid the shortcomings and display the talents of the actors of his company, so he planned them to exploit the assets and avoid the defects of his theater.

Though he wrote more plays for the first Globe than

for any other playhouse, he planned plays for at least three other houses—The Theatre, the Curtain, and Blackfriars—and with all his theatrical experience he pretty surely made adjustments to fit his plays to different houses. These adjustments we cannot yet fully perceive, however, because we are still too uncertain of the precise dates of many of the plays and too unsure of the precise differences between the various theaters.

In general we know that the theaters found in late sixteenth- and early seventeenth-century London appeared in two forms: public theaters like The Theatre, the Curtain, the Swan, the Globe, the Fortune, and the Red Bull, and private theaters like Blackfriars, the Phoenix, and the Salisbury Court. Both kinds were in use during Shakespeare's years in London, but his company did not perform in a private playhouse before 1609. Though he may well have written most of his late plays—*Cymbeline, The Winter's Tale, The Tempest,* and *The Two Noble Kinsmen*—to be performed at Blackfriars, a private theater, nearly nine-tenths of his dramatic output was designed for presentation in his company's public theaters, The Theatre, the Curtain, and the Globe. It is, therefore, the general characteristics of these public theaters and their audiences that Shakespeare had in mind for most of his plays.

During his working years the audience at the public theaters was large in size and mixed in character. There are only two known contemporary estimates of the capacity of Elizabethan public theaters, one made by a touring Dutchman named Johannes de Witt, who visited the Swan Theatre in 1596, and the other made by the Spanish Ambassador, who reported to his government about the size of the crowds at the Globe Theatre at several performances of a smash hit play in the summer of 1625. Both men name the same capacity figure: 3,000.

These large public theater audiences were, during most of Shakespeare's lifetime, surprisingly mixed in their components. Since the public theaters offered a variety of accommodation—from standing room in the pit, bought for a general admission fee of one penny (later twopence), to semisecluded private rooms in the galleries at many times the general admission fee—the audience included both extremes of the social scale as well as the middle-income group in the galleries priced intermediately. Such an audience—a cross-section of the London populace—is one of the distinctive characteristics of the Elizabethan dramatic milieu; it has never been duplicated since. At a single performance of a popular play like *Richard II* there might be pickpockets, prostitutes, apprentices, sailors, petty tradesmen, brewers, students, lawyers, members of parliament, landed gentlemen, courtiers, public officials, and great noblemen; all these types are mentioned in one contemporary reference or another as appearing in the public theater audience. The great variety of appeal in most Elizabethan public theater plays, including Shakespeare's, was evidently elicited in part by the great diversity of spectators.

These public theaters were polygonal in shape, with covered galleries (three in all specified instances) runing around the inside. The center area, called the pit, was unroofed and provided only standing room. The stage was a platform which jutted out into this pit. The only extant precise specifications call for a platform to extend to the middle of the pit, making an open stage area of 43 feet by 27½ feet. Behind this platform were the stage entrances from the "tiring house," as the dressing rooms were called. The part of the gallery which ran behind the platform was frequently used as part of the stage when the action required an elevated situation. Beneath this balcony was a curtained space—probably demountable in some of the public theaters—in which the few scenes that required sudden revelations to the audience could be arranged. The major acting area, however, was the platform; the balcony and the curtained place, in modern studies often called the "inner stage," were for occasional use; some plays did not require them at all.

These characteristic features of Elizabethan theaters are more fully set forth in A. M. Nagler's *Shakespeare's Stage,* where they can be examined in detail. Here it is more relevant to consider the formative influence the general features of Shakespeare's playhouse had upon his preparation of scenes.

An examination of the general plan of the Elizabethan public theaters will make it apparent that though they held a much larger audience than the average London and New York theater of today, the bulk of the audience was nevertheless closer to the actors than in our present-day theaters. This apparent contradiction is explained by the disposition of the audience in playhouses like the Globe. Our usual theaters, in their cubic form, consist of a small box (the stage) set beside and opening into a large box (the auditorium). The audience is spread over the floor of the large box and on one or two shelves (balconies) at the back of the large box. This plan requires that most of the space within the cubic form of our theaters be devoted to empty air, and that the actors "project" their lines and effects out of the small box into the large one.

As we have seen, the cubic plan of the Elizabethan theater was different. Instead of two boxes, there was only one box, in which both actors and audience were together. More of the air space was filled because the three shelves or balconies completely circled the inside of the auditorium, and the balcony audience was stacked all around the box instead of being shoved to the back. The audience on the floor of the Elizabethan auditorium had no seats; it stood, and could therefore be packed in three or four times as many to the square yard of floor space as in our seated auditoriums. Finally, the actors, instead of being off in a separate box, were on a platform stage which extended from the back to the middle of the house, and the actor who was downstage had spectators completely surrounding him in the balconies and almost surrounding him on the auditorium floor. He did not have to "project" through the proscenium opening from the box of the stage into the box of the auditorium but could act from the middle of the house to auditors conveniently standing all about him; the most distant spectator in the back of the topmost balcony was actually closer to him than the most distant spectator in the last row of the balcony in our smaller theaters.

The concentrated grouping of the Elizabethan public theater audience and the consequent shortening of the distance between the downstage actor and the most remote of the spectators made possible more intimate effects and more rapid transitions from mood to mood than can be easily attained in our proscenium arch theaters. Similarly, since the Elizabethan public theaters used neither sets nor intermissions between scenes, cumulative effects from scene to scene were commonly attained to a degree that is impossible in our playhouses. We can, of course, remember during Act II what happened in Act I, but we can only dimly recapture the mood of Act I after it has been interrupted by the fall of the curtain, the brightening of the lights, the intermission smoke, and the desultory conversation which has, for a few minutes, completely broken our absorption in the make-believe of the play. Modern playwrights, therefore, cannot carry over their effects from scene to scene as Shakespeare did, but must begin to develop the mood and the concentration all over again after each intermission break.

This cumulation and continuity of effect in the Elizabethan theater were further facilitated by the regular use of the three playing areas of the stage. The first and most important was the open projecting platform where the great majority of the action took place. The second was an inner enclosed space where heavy properties could be arranged or actors could be set for a sudden revelation, as indicated by the stage direction in the fifth act of *The Tempest:*

> *Here Prospero discouers Ferdinand and Miranda, playing at Chesse.*

The third playing area was an elevated place in the balcony behind the platform from which characters could speak down to actors below them, as Juliet does from her window or balcony to Romeo in the orchard beneath, or as King Richard II does from the walls of Flint Castle to Bolingbroke on the ground below. This flexible stage made possible uninterrupted action, as when, after 125 lines spoken from the walls, King Richard comes down and, without any break in continuity, continues with Bolingbroke in the "base court."

These features of Elizabethan playhouses like the Globe gave Shakespeare three great assets unfamiliar in normal modern theaters and only occasionally available in experimental ones: flexibility, speed, and intimacy of effect. Flexibility made possible the nineteen changes of scene in *Hamlet* with no greater delay or loss of concentration than if every scene had been written for the same background. Speed made possible the delivery of the 3,900 lines of *Hamlet* in about three hours, whereas modern productions of the play must either cut out one-third of the lines, as they generally

134

do, or run for about four hours, as the few uncut productions of *Hamlet* have done. Intimacy of effect, which Shakespeare knew the actors of the Lord Chamberlain's company could get at the Globe, made easy the speaking of soliloquies and asides that are awkward and sometimes completely ludicrous in modern proscenium-arch theaters.

Shakespeare knew that on the stage of the Globe the actor in *Hamlet* who had an aside coming up could maneuver clear downstage where at the edge of the platform he had a hundred or more spectators crowded round the stage and much closer to him than the other actors, who would be upstage and as much as thirty or forty feet away. Thus in Act II, Scene 2, Hamlet is pacing to and fro reading a book when Polonius approaches him at line 171. They talk for sixteen lines, during which Hamlet can work upstage while Polonius maneuvers downstage, so that when the time comes for Polonius' aside to the audience:

> How say you by that? Still harping on my daughter. Yet he knew me not at first; 'a said I was a fishmonger. 'A is far gone . . .

he can speak directly and easily to the audience, some of whom are close enough for him to reach out and touch, while Hamlet, still reading his book, has walked upstage far enough away to seem out of earshot.

Perhaps we can use *Hamlet* again to make a little clearer Shakespeare's dependence upon the flexibility and speed made possible by the structure of the Globe for the attainment of effects at the beginning of the play. He has planned his opening scene to take place on an upper level, which the audience, even without the aid of programs, will soon perceive to be the sentinels' platform at a castle. The tone set by this scene is important for the play. It develops an atmosphere

of cold, of foreboding, and of fear. All three of the sentinels are frightened, so frightened that the wrong man
challenges in the first three lines of the play. Their
alarm and apprehension are conveyed to the audience
by their hushed excited tones and then by the actual
appearance of the Ghost, which they have been fearing
all the time and which will not speak to them. This
fear, this sense of foreboding, is important for the
whole play. It must be transferred to Hamlet and carried on to the rest of the action. The audience must
have a vivid memory of the cold and dark and sinister
Scene 1 as they watch the bustle and brilliance of Scene
2, where the whole court assembles.

At the Globe this carry-over of the memory and
mood of Scene 1 into Scene 2 was easy, for there was
no interruption, no break of the audience's concentrated attention between scenes. Horatio at the end
of Scene 1 says,

> Let us impart what we have seen to-night
> Unto young Hamlet, for, upon my life,
> This spirit, dumb to us, will speak to him.
> Do you consent we shall acquaint him with it,
> As needful in our loves, fitting our duty?
> MAR. Let's do't, I pray; and I this morning know
> Where we shall find him most conveniently.

At the same moment as the three sentinels walk off
the upper stage, King Claudius, Queen Gertrude, Hamlet, Polonius, and all the court walk on below. At the
Globe there was no pause of any kind. The audience
shifted its gaze from the disappearing sentinels above
to the entering court below, identifying the King and
Queen by their robes and crowns and by their position
in the procession, and Hamlet as the Prince by his position immediately after the King and Queen, as befitted

his rank as the third most honored person in the kingdom. He has indeed been found "most conveniently."

Speed and flexibility are vital here. It is important
that as King Claudius speaks the opening lines of the
second scene—

> Though yet of Hamlet our dear brother's death
> The memory be green—

the audience should still be thinking of the ghost of
this "dear brother" walking the battlements in the cold
night. The dishonesty of his first speech before his
court is nicely concealed, but if the audience has never
had its concentrated attention broken since seeing the
Ghost, it will inevitably suspect his sincerity, though it
will not quite know why. In our modern theaters this
carry-over effect is almost impossible to get, because,
however swiftly the transition between scenes is handled, the audience has a few distracting seconds to
break its attention on some irrelevant sight—the des-
cending curtain, or the opening transverse, or even
the changing lights, and this break in concentration
is enough to dilute or destroy the important mood of
Scene 1 before the court has entered.

The speed and continuity of performance for which
Shakespeare and his contemporary dramatists planned
the production of their plays are also facilitated by the
essentially placeless character of their drama, a characteristic which commonly makes trouble for modern
readers and modern producers. For more than two
centuries now, European and American drama has
been a drama of place, and the convention has become
so firmly established that it seldom occurs to most
theater-goers that anything else is possible, or that our
stage sets are a convention. We naturally assume that
every dramatist has always imagined each episode in

his play as occurring at some particular place—a bedroom, a bar, a garden, a restaurant, a battlement, or a dungeon—and we are encouraged in this erroneous assumption by the staging all too frequently used in modern productions of the plays of Shakespeare and his contemporaries—in which we watch the actors perform in a set suggesting a street in Venice, or a great hall in a castle, or a woodland glade. Furthermore, nearly all modern editions of Shakespeare's plays print at the head of every scene a statement about place: "*A Room in* Duke Frederick's *Palace,*" "*Elsinore. A room in the house of* Polonius," "*Venice. The street before* Shylock's *house.*" All such statements are eighteenth- or nineteenth-century inventions, not Shakespeare's words.

No edition of a play of Shakespeare's published in his lifetime had any indication of place printed at the head of any scene; none of the many seventeenth-century editions published after his death added any such statement. Indeed, none of the seventeenth-century editions ever fully divided all the plays into acts and scenes, and a number of plays, like *Antony and Cleopatra* and *Romeo and Juliet,* were published in the seventeenth century with no act or scene divisions at all. The now familiar system of localizing all scenes in Shakespeare's plays was begun by Nicholas Rowe in his edition of 1709 and more or less completed by Lewis Theobald in 1733 and Sir Thomas Hanmer in 1744.

The theater of Rowe's time, for which he wrote his own plays and in which his readers saw Shakespeare's produced, was a type of playhouse more resembling ours than Shakespeare's. Sets were regularly used, so Rowe invented places in which he thought the scenes of Shakespeare's plays should take place, and for early eighteenth-century readers and play-goers these suggested settings, since they conformed to the accustomed place convention, seemed not only normal but inevitable. Unfortunately they involve a violent contradiction of the principle which governed Shakespeare and his fellow dramatists when they wrote for the Elizabethan public theaters.

Theirs was a drama of persons, not a drama of places. The plan of their theaters with its provisions for intimate contact between actors and audience and for various angles of vision made the actor paramount and his background only occasionally significant. In the majority of scenes in Elizabethan plays the audience is expected to concentrate wholly on words and action and to ignore the place where the action may have occurred. Indeed it is apparent that in most scenes the dramatist himself had not thought about the place; what Othello and Iago said to each other and how they acted as they said it are important, not where the encounter took place.

When Nicholas Rowe and succeeding editors of the eighteenth century concluded that they must nominate a setting for each episode in every play of Shakespeare, they simply read through each play carefully looking for hints of place. In the first scene of *Othello,* for instance, this was easy enough. Though the first 73 lines make no reference to place and could have occurred in almost any spot where Iago and Roderigo could be alone, at line 74 Roderigo says, "Here is her father's house. I'll call aloud." So, thought Lewis Theobald, they must have been talking in front of Brabantio's house, and the front of a house would be on a street. Therefore in his edition he inserted at the beginning of the play, "Act I Scene *a Street in* Venice."

The following scene, however, is harder. The only reference to a proximate place is Othello's agreement to go with Cassio and the officers:

> I will but spend a word here in the house,
> And go with you.

Othello seems to be in the house to which he has brought Desdemona. But there are three entrances "with Torches" in the scene, and they would seem inappropriate indoors. To Theobald a street again seemed to be the solution, but it could not be the same street as in Scene 1, because 25 lines before the end of that scene Iago had left Roderigo, telling him to bring Brabantio and the searchers to find Othello:

> Lead to the *Saggitary* the raised search
> And there will I be with him.

Therefore just above the entrance of Othello and Iago, Theobald inserted his solution to the localization problem: "SCENE *changes to another Street, before the* Sagittary." And most editors have been following Theobald's insertion in some form ever since.

Such determined efforts to localize the setting for hundreds of scenes in Shakespeare's plays have seemed legitimate and helpful to readers of the plays for more than two centuries now because the place statements accord with their ideas of how plays are planned and acted. Unfortunately Elizabethan plays were not planned and acted according to the conventions of the eighteenth- and nineteenth-century theater, and these insistent localizations often spoil the effects that Shakespeare and his contemporary playwrights designed. The disturbing fact is that Shakespeare thought of most of the scenes in his plays as taking place on the outer stage, or perhaps the upper stage, of the Globe Theatre and he did not suggest to his audience any background at all until a specific place became useful for his action, and then he called attention to it.

A play most seriously mutilated by insistence on

modern practice is *Antony and Cleopatra,* which had no act and scene divisions in any seventeenth-century edition. Nicholas Rowe, however, divided it into 27 scenes, and Sir Thomas Hanmer in his edition of 1744 further divided it into 42 scenes, carefully numbered and located. Hanmer's numbered divisions are followed and his localizations accepted and even extended in nearly all editions down to our own time, thus breaking up the flowing action into fragments extremely difficult to stage under our conventions and irritating and confusing to a conventional modern reader who tries to change the imagined background to a different place thirty or forty different times in the course of the tragedy.

Another example of the distortion which misunderstanding of the conventions of place as Shakespeare handled them can be found in the first 233 lines of the second act of *Romeo and Juliet.* In none of the many editions of the play before 1700 had this second act been divided into scenes. In all of them, after the chorus or prologue that follows the Capulet ball, Romeo enters alone and speaks two lines. Benvolio and Mercutio come in calling for Romeo; they do not see him, and they continue to call for him and to talk about him for 40 lines, at the end of which they give up and leave to go home and to bed. As soon as they leave, Romeo, having heard all they said, makes a one-line comment on their talk; he then sees Juliet appear at the window or balcony above and begins to discourse on her without further reference to Benvolio and Mercutio. Juliet speaks, and there follows the famous dialogue of "the first balcony scene," in the course of which they say:

> JUL. How cam'st thou hither, tell me, and wherefore?

The orchard walls are high and hard to climb,
And the place death, considering who thou art,
If any of my kinsmen find thee here.

> ROM. With Love's light wings did I o'erperch
> these walls.

And so on, to Juliet's final exit, above, and Romeo's exit, below. From Romeo's first entrance to the statement of his resolve to seek out Friar Lawrence's assistance, there is no break in the flow of the action.

For Rowe's stage with its literal representation of place, this sequence of actions presented a problem. Clearly, he thought, Romeo in his first two lines and Benvolio and Mercutio in the next forty must have been on their way home from the Capulet ball, and their way home must have been along a street or lane. But for the "balcony scene" Juliet must have been at a window or balcony of the Capulet house and Romeo must have been below her in the Capulet orchard *inside* the high orchard walls to which Juliet refers. Obviously, according to the conventions of Rowe's theater, this action involved two separate scenes. But according to Shakespeare's text Romeo never leaves the stage.

Trying to make the best of what seemed to him a bad situation, Rowe broke up the lines into different scenes and added locations and the stage directions that he thought necessary. Successive eighteenth-century editors elaborated what he had done until the place designation at the beginning of the scene reads,

A lane by the wall of Capulet's *orchard.*

After two lines of this scene, a stage direction for Romeo was inserted:

Climbs the wall and leaps down within it.

Then after the exeunt of Benvolio and Mercutio at line 42, the scene was broken off and another was indicated with a new entrance:

Scene II. Capulet's *orchard*. *Enter* Romeo.

This series of alterations and insertions takes care of the problem according to eighteenth- and nineteenth-century conventions of staging, and it is still used in most modern editions of the play. But none of the additions are Shakespeare's, and they spoil the effect he designed. As Shakespeare planned the action of his play for a characteristic Elizabethan public theater presentation, the first balcony scene was a statement of the freshness and beauty of young love, and the poignant innocence of Juliet and Romeo—superbly expressed in their love duet—has become the most famous of all such statements in dramatic literature. But Shakespeare planned to heighten the effect of the episode by strong contrast—a favorite method of most of the Elizabethan playwrights. The first movement of his scene is dominated by the virile Mercutio conjuring up the lost Romeo with shouted innuendoes about his erstwhile mistress Rosaline. Against such a background of entertaining young masculine bawdry, the eloquent and moving innocence of the balcony scene will gain much, but for the full effect there must be no break at all between the first and second movements of the scene—bawdry must merge into innocence as Juliet appears:

> But soft, what light through yonder window breaks?
> It is the East and Juliet is the sun.

As the scene was planned for the Elizabethan stage, the setting for the first 43 lines was no place or any place. After his first two lines Romeo conceals himself at any convenient place on the stage, from which he emerges as Benvolio and Mercutio leave. The stage is still no place until Juliet appears and Romeo says "yonder window," when it becomes the ground outside the Capulet house, and then, more specifically, the Capulet orchard. There is no wall in sight, and at the end of the scene Romeo walks off normally, as he had walked on, planting in the minds of the audience the information that the next scene will be localized by saying,

> Hence will I to my ghostly Friar's close cell,
> His help to crave and my dear hap to tell.

Shakespeare has even emphasized the fact that lines 1–42 and lines 43–233 are two movements of the same scene and not Scenes 1 and 2 by making the departing Benvolio and the emerging Romeo divide the two lines of a couplet between them, as Romeo and Juliet had done in the previous scene at the Capulet ball.

> BEN.   Go then, for 'tis in vain
> To seek him here that means not to be found.

> ROM. He jests at scars that never felt a wound.

And Romeo's line in the couplet is a comment on the talk of Mercutio and Benvolio that has made up the introductory movement of the scene.

Shakespeare's plays contain many such examples of his exploitation of the convention of the placeless stage. His observation of this convention, like his consideration for the size of his company, for the talents and limitations of his men and boy actors, and for the structural possibilities of his theater, are aspects of his direction of his genius as a playwright and poet into the forms of the theater and the acting company that he knew so much better than any other dramatist of his time.

CHAPTER 6

The Nondramatic Poet

THOUGH Shakespeare's great achievement is that
of the playwright unsurpassed, his first writing to appear in print was a long poem called *Venus and Adonis,* which the printer Richard Field, a Stratford boy
who had come to London several years before Shakespeare, entered in the Stationers' Register on 18 April
1593 and printed in the same year. On the title page
of the book no author's name appears, but for the following page Shakespeare has written a dedication—a
thing he never did for any of his plays:

> To The Right Honorable Henrie
> Wriothesley, Earle of Southampton, and
> Baron of Titchfield.

> Right Honourable, I know not how I shall of-
> fend in dedicating my vnpolisht lines to your Lord-
> ship, nor how the worlde will censure mee for
> choosing so strong a proppe to support so weake
> a burthen, onelye if your Honour seeme but
> pleased, I account my selfe highly praised, and
> vowe to take aduantage of all idle houres, till I
> haue honoured you with some grauer labour. But
> if the first heire of my inuention proue deformed,

I shall be sorie it had so noble a god-father: and neuer after eare so barren a land, for feare it yeeld me still so bad a haruest, I leaue it to your Honourable suruey, and your Honor to your hearts content which I wish may alwaies answere your owne wish, and the worlds hopefull expectation.
Your Honors in all dutie,
William Shakespeare.

The phrases in this dedication have often been misinterpreted by modern readers, who are much more aware of Shakespeare's plays than of his poems and who are unfamiliar with the differing degrees of respect which the Elizabethans ordinarily accorded to plays in the theater and to poems in print. The very tone of the dedication, which would seem unctuous and subservient if written now, was normal enough in the 1590's; indeed, many extant volumes of the time have dedications far more flattering than this one. The phrase "the first heire of my inuention" does not mean "my first composition," as might be assumed, but "my first work brought to publication." A number of Shakespeare's plays had been written and acted before this dedication was composed, but none had been published; *Venus and Adonis* was the first work he had composed for readers and the first to appear in print. His resolve that he will "neuer after eare so barren a land" if this "first heire of my inuention proue deformed" does not indicate that he proposes to stop writing if *Venus and Adonis* should prove a failure but only that such a failure would deter him from sending more poems to the printer. As in so much that he did, Shakespeare's phrasing in this dedication reflects the common assumption of the time that plays written for theater audiences and literature printed for readers are in quite different categories.

Since the printer of *Venus and Adonis* had the manuscript licensed for publication on 18 April 1593, it is likely that Shakespeare had written the poem during the preceding nine or ten months when plague had closed all the theaters and most actors were unemployed. The poem itself is a long narrative—1194 lines —of the Ovidian type, and though it is far from his greatest it was for many years one of Shakespeare's most popular works; during his lifetime it was reprinted more often than anything else he wrote.

Gabriel Harvey, the Cambridge friend of Edmund Spenser, wrote perceptively in the margin of his copy of Chaucer's works,

> The younger sort takes much delight in Shakespeares Venus, & Adonis: but his Lucrece, & his tragedie of Hamlet, Prince of Denmarke, haue it in them, to please the wiser sort.

John Weever's poem *Ad Guglielmum Shakespeare* is an excellent example of the popularity of *Venus and Adonis* with the "younger sort"; published in 1599, when Weever was twenty-three, it begins:

> Honie-tong'd *Shakespeare* when I saw thine issue
> I swore *Apollo* got them and none other,
> Their rosie-tainted features cloth'd in tissue,
> Some heauen born goddesse said to be their
> mother:
> Rose-checkt *Adonis* with his amber tresses,
> Faire fire-hot *Venus* charming him to loue her.

Similarly the Cambridge students who wrote the *Parnassus* plays (see above, pp. 108–10) reflected the popularity of *Venus and Adonis* with youth. In the first part of *The Returne from Parnassus,* acted at St. John's College, Cambridge, probably toward the end of the Christmas season of 1599, the character Gullio, a pretender to military skills and literary taste, asks to have verses written for him to give to his mistress for New Year's Day:

> . . . make mee them in two or three diuers vayns, in Chaucers, Gowers and Spencers, and Mr Shakspeares. Marry I thinke I shall entertaine those verses which run like these:
>> Euen as the sunn with purple coloured face
>> Had tane his laste leaue on the weeping morne, etc.
>> [*Venus and Adonis*, lines 1–2]
> O sweet Mr Shakspeare, Ile haue his picture in my study at the courte.

And in the next scene, after the commissioned verses in imitation of Shakespeare have been read to him, Gullio exclaims:

> Noe more, I am one that can iudge accordinge to the proverbe *bouem ex vnguibus*. Ey marry S^r, these haue some life in them: let this duncified worlde esteeme of Spĕcer and Chaucer, Ile worshipp sweet Mr Shakspeare, and to honoure him will lay his *Venus and Adonis* vnder my pillowe, as wee reade of one (I do not well remember his name, but I am sure he was a kinge) slept with Homer vnder his beds heade.

Perhaps the praise of a character like Gullio, who had quoted and paraphrased *Venus and Adonis* before in the play, indicates that the authors of the play did not hold the poem in highest esteem, but their easy use of it demonstrates clearly that they relied on their Cambridge audience to have an intimate knowledge of the poem, to recognize the lines, and to know the author.

One year after *Venus and Adonis* had been licensed for publication and entered in the Stationers' Register, Shakespeare had a second long narrative poem ready. *The Rape of Lucrece* is so similar to *Venus and Adonis* in style and genre and circumstances of publication that the two are usually referred to together, and they share what might be called a common history. Both were apparently written during the long and devastating epidemic of the plague from the summer of 1592 to the late spring of 1594, during which the theaters were closed and the actors almost constantly out of work. Both were printed by Richard Field, formerly of Stratford, though for *Lucrece* he was printer only, whereas he had been both printer and publisher of *Venus and Adonis*. Both texts are much more free from error than those of any other printed works of Shakespeare, an indication that for them he carefully read proof, though he never did so for the printed texts of any of his plays. Both were printed without an author's name on the title page, though they are certainly Shakespeare's, for his name appears in full after the dedications—dedications which again set these two pieces together and apart from Shakespeare's other works, because for these poems alone in the entire canon did he make any such presentation. And finally, the poems are both addressed to the same man.

The dedication to *Venus and Adonis* we have seen. The dedication to *The Rape of Lucrece* reads:

> To the Right Honovrable, Henry Wriothesley, Earle of Southhampton, and Baron of Titchfield.
> The loue I dedicate to your Lordship is without end: wherof this Pamphlet without beginning is but a superfluous Moity. The warrant I haue of your Honourable disposition, not the worth of my

vntutord Lines makes it assured of acceptance.
What I haue done is yours, what I haue to doe is
yours, being part in all I haue, deuoted yours.
Were my worth greater, my duety would shew
greater, meane time, as it is, it is bound to your
Lordship; To whom I wish long life still lengthned
with all happinesse.

> Your Lordships in all duety.
> William Shakespeare.

These dedications represent a practice common
among nondramatic poets but one exceedingly rare
at the time among playwrights, who normally sold
their plays to the acting companies to be performed
and not to the printers to be published. It is not really
surprising, therefore, that among the seventy-odd issues
or editions of Shakespeare's various writings that were
published during his lifetime, only the issues of *Venus
and Adonis* and *The Rape of Lucrece* have dedications.

The relationship of Shakespeare and his patron has
been a popular subject for speculation and heated de-
bate for two centuries. Much of the discussion, which
has decreased somewhat of late but certainly has not
disappeared, has derived from a misconception of the
position of the poet as compared to that of the playwright in the time, and to an exaggerated notion of the
unlearned country innocence of the young Shakespeare. Many fine imaginative stories of Southampton's
introduction of Shakespeare into noble and courtly
circles and of the influence of Southampton's various
troubles on Shakespeare's plays have been invented
and retailed with conviction. Actually the only evidence that exists to show that Shakespeare ever had
anything to do with Southampton or ever sought pa-
tronage from him exists in the dedications of the two
poems in 1593 and 1594. The first is tentatively worded

and seems to indicate slight acquaintance with the Earl; the second is more assured; after this there is no clear evidence of any relationship between the two men at all.

Even if the association were brief, however, we are interested in the poet's patron, and because of his position we know a fair amount about him. When Shakespeare dedicated *Venus and Adonis* to him in 1593, Henry Wriothesley, third Earl of Southampton and Baron Titchfield, was nineteen years old. He had become heir to the Southampton title, estates, and debts at the age of eight, and as minor heir of a great estate he was a ward of the Queen. Lord Burghley, Lord High Treasurer of England and principal minister of Elizabeth, acted as his guardian before he came of age. A marriage with Elizabeth Vere, daughter of the Earl of Oxford and granddaughter of Lord Burghley, seems to have been arranged, but in 1594, when he was twenty, the young Earl secured a release from the engagement by paying a large forfeit of £5,000. In 1595 he began an intrigue with Elizabeth Vernon, a cousin of the Earl of Essex and a maid of honor of Queen Elizabeth; the intrigue came to light in 1598 when they were secretly married three months before the birth of their daughter, and for a time both the Earl and his wife were imprisoned for their contempt of the Queen. Southampton was devoted to the Earl of Essex, his wife's cousin and one of Queen Elizabeth's favorites; he went on several naval and military expeditions with him, he was with Essex during his disastrous campaign in Ireland in 1599, and in 1601 he was sentenced to death for his part in the Essex rebellion. Though Essex was executed, Southampton's sentence was commuted to life imprisonment, and he was released when James I succeeded Elizabeth in 1603. He died in Holland in 1624.

The great interest in the possible relation of this rather ungovernable young man with Shakespeare is not centered in the fact that *Venus and Adonis* and *The Rape of Lucrece* were dedicated to him but in the speculation suggested by these dedications that Southampton was the young man to whom Shakespeare wrote a number of sonnets, which the speculators assume to be autobiographical. In the last 200 years much ink has been spilled in worrying this thesis. The volume of Shakespeare's sonnets therefore, though it was not published until fifteen and sixteen years after the two narrative poems had appeared, requires discussion with them.

During the first thirty-five years of Shakespeare's life the writing of sonnets—a form developed in Italy and France centuries before and widely practiced there throughout the sixteenth century—became more and more popular in England, until in the last decade of the century so many of them were published that one can call their vogue a sonneteering rage. Many hundreds of single sonnets were written, but especially notable in this decade are the cycles, or series of sonnets, more or less unified by their address to a beloved woman or sometimes to a man and purporting to set forth a story or the development of a personal relationship.

Shakespeare wrote a number of separate sonnets that are incorporated into plays—*Love's Labour's Lost, Romeo and Juliet, Henry V, All's Well That Ends Well* all contain them—but the phrase "Shakespeare's sonnets" normally refers to the 154 in the collection published in 1609 under that title. Though there has long been disagreement about the dates at which they were written, some of them had been passed about in manuscript at least as early as 1598, when Francis Meres in his *Palladis Tamia,* published in that year, patriotically compared a number of English poets to Greek and Roman poets:

> As the soule of *Euphorbus* was thought to liue in *Pythagoras:* so the sweete wittie soule of *Ouid* liues in mellifluous & hony-tongued *Shakespeare,* witnes his *Venus* and *Adonis,* his *Lucrece,* his sugred Sonnets among his priuate friends, &c.

In spite of enthusiastic efforts to prove that Shakespeare wrote most of his sonnets in the late eighties, most scholars now agree that at least the bulk of them was written in the 1590's.

The collection was not published, however, until 1609, when the publisher Thomas Thorpe had George Eld print them for him. By this time the great vogue of sonneteering had been over for a decade, and many considered the form old-fashioned or even ridiculous. Shakespeare evidently had nothing to do with the printing of Thorpe's volume, for he wrote no dedication, as he had for his two previous nondramatic publications, and the book has many misprints so obvious that not even a competent proofreader, much less an author, could have missed them all.

The book does have a dedication, for Thomas Thorpe himself wrote one that has puzzled readers ever since.

TO·THE·ONLIE·BEGETTER·OF·
THESE·INSVING·SONNETS·
M.ʳ W. H. ALL·HAPPINESSE·
AND·THAT·ETERNITIE·
PROMISED·
BY·
OUR·EVER-LIVING·POET·
WISHETH·
THE·WELL-WISHING·
ADVENTVRER·IN·
SETTING·
FORTH·
T.T.

Who is "M⸢r⸣ W. H."? Does Thomas Thorpe mean
that he was the man who procured the manuscript of
the sonnets for him, or does he mean that W.H. was
the man for whom the sonnets were written? Most
writers about Shakespeare have assumed the latter, but
there is no agreement on who he might have been; not
unnaturally, the most popular candidate has been the
Earl of Southampton, because of the earlier dedications
of *Venus and Adonis* and *The Rape of Lucrece*. Unfortunately he was not "Mr.," but an Earl and a Baron,
as he had been when Shakespeare addressed him by
these titles in *Venus and Adonis* sixteen years before.
And the initials of his family name were not W.H.,
but H.W.

At this point the character of the sonnets becomes
relevant. The 154 that Thorpe published in 1609 are
somewhat miscellaneous in subject, but they fall into
three groups. The first seventeen are addressed to a
young man who is urged to marry; the next 109 are
varied in subject and the majority seem to be addressed
to a man, though many of them could have been addressed to anybody or nobody; most, but not all, of the
last twenty-eight are addressed to or written about a
woman or women. Some of the sonnets appear to refer
to events that may be either real or fictitious, and many
accounts have been published, usually wildly imaginative, in attempts to fit these events into the life of
Shakespeare and the life of the writer's favorite candidate for the young man to whom the first seventeen are
addressed. After the Earl of Southampton, the most
popular names have been William Herbert, Earl of
Pembroke; Robert Devereux, Earl of Essex; and plain
William Hughes.

All this is the purest speculation. If a number of
Shakespeare's sonnets were addressed to a real man and
not a fictitious one, no one knows who he was, and at

this late date we are not likely to find out. If any of the episodes in personal relationships alluded to in the sonnets are real instead of imaginary, they are unlikely to be identified now, and certainly no such suggested episodes can be made part of a Shakespeare biography simply on the grounds of a clouded image appearing in the sonnets. In spite of the thousands of pages that have been written on the Earl of Southampton as the poet's patron, the only *facts* so far established are Shakespeare's dedication of two long poems to him in 1593 and 1594.

Venus and Adonis, The Rape of Lucrece, and *The Sonnets* are, then, Shakespeare's principal nondramatic works, but there are several other publications in which his compositions form a part, or are said to. Some of them are clearly publishers' fraudulent attempts to capitalize on Shakespeare's growing reputation, but two preserve poems of which Shakespeare's authorship is a still-debated possibility.

In 1599 William Jaggard published two editions (the first of which is known only from a unique fragment) of a small volume whose title page reads "The Passionate Pilgrime. By W. Shakespeare." The little book contains twenty independent poems, of which five are his and most of the remainder are certainly not. Poems iii, v, and xvi are taken from the fourth act of *Love's Labour's Lost,* which had been published the previous year; they are the poems written in the play by Don Armado, Longaville, and Dumain. Poems i and ii are sonnets printed ten years later in the edition of 1609 as cxxxviii and cxliv; since they had not been published before the appearance of *The Passionate Pilgrim,* Jaggard must have got them from some manuscript now lost. Of the other poems published in the volume as Shakespeare's, two or three were written by Richard Barnfield; one is probably by Marlowe, with a reply by

Sir Walter Raleigh; one is by Thomas Deloney; one, and perhaps three others, by Bartholomew Griffin; and half a dozen were written by unknown authors; but there is no good reason to think that Shakespeare wrote any of them.

In 1612 Jaggard brought out an expanded edition of *The Passionate Pilgrim* with the elaborated title:

> The Passionate Pilgrime. Or Certaine Amorous Sonnets, betweene Venus and Adonis, newly corrected and augmented. By W. Shakespere. The third Edition. Whereunto is newly added two Loue-Epistles, the first from Paris to Hellen, and Hellens answere backe againe to Paris.

The added material consists of nine poems by Thomas Heywood lifted from his *Troia Britanica*, which Jaggard himself had published three years before, a "dishonesty" against which Heywood published a protest. In spite of the title-page claims, the new edition of *The Passionate Pilgrim* has nothing to do with Shakespeare's *Venus and Adonis*. These facts are enough to demonstrate Jaggard's fraudulent intentions and the advertising value which he assumed Shakespeare's name and the title of his poem to have.

The most curious and enigmatic of the poems attributed to Shakespeare appears in a book published in 1601 with the involved title,

> Loues Martyr: Or, Rosalins Complaint. Allegorically shadowing the truth of Loue, in the constant Fate of the Phœnix and Turtle. A Poeme enterlaced with much varietie and raritie; now first translated out of the venerable Italian Torquato Cæliano, by Robert Chester . . . To these are added some new compositions, of seuerall moderne Writers whose names are subscribed to their seuerall

workes, vpon the first Subiect: viz. the Phœnix and Turtle.

The second part of the volume, following Chester's "Love's Martyr," consists of eight poems signed variously "Vatum Chorus" (2), "Ignoto," "William Shakespeare," "John Marston," "George Chapman," and "Ben Johnson" (2). The poem over Shakespeare's name, generally called "The Phoenix and the Turtle," consists of thirteen quatrains and a concluding "Threnos" of five three-line stanzas. The purpose and meaning of the poem are obscure, and there is no general agreement as to its interpretation. Various critics have denied that Shakespeare wrote the poem, generally on the grounds that they did not think it good enough for him, but there is really no compelling reason for either rejecting or accepting it.

Finally there is a 329-line pastoral poem written in the seven-line stanzas used in *Lucrece;* it consists of a lament by a maiden over her betrayal by a deceitful lover and is entitled "A Lover's Complaint." The poem was first published by Thomas Thorpe in 1609 at the end of his edition of Shakespeare's sonnets. There is no evidence except Thorpe's attribution for assigning the poem to Shakespeare, and though the attribution may be correct, many critics have doubted it.

A collection of Shakespeare's nondramatic poetry, presumably intended to be complete and alleged by the publisher to be authentic, appeared in 1640. The volume, entitled "Poems: Written By Wil. Shake-speare. Gent." was printed by Thomas Cotes for the publisher John Benson. Actually it is a scissors-and-paste job which confused Shakespeare's editors for 200 years and which even now sometimes misleads the gullible, who are inclined to assign some significance to Benson's irresponsible rearranging and appropriating.

The only new Shakespearean material in it is a portrait of the author that William Marshall engraved from the one in the First Folio, a misleading address to the reader by John Benson, a new poem to Shakespeare's memory by Leonard Digges, and another by John Warren. The rest of the book is nearly all taken from previously printed volumes to most of which Benson had no rights. But Benson, or someone working for him, has had great fun scrambling the poems so that at first sight they give no clue as to what they really are. There are 146 of the 154 sonnets from the 1609 edition, but they have been ingeniously disguised by printing them all out of order; by combining two, three, four, or even five sonnets into one poem; by making up titles for each set of rearranged sonnets; and by interspersing among them all the poems from the 1612 *Passionate Pilgrim,* whether Shakespeare's or not. Then come nine poems including two lyrics from *Measure for Measure* and *As You Like It,* three elegies on Shakespeare's death, and four additional poems by other writers. At this point Benson prints "Finis," but he adds another section headed "An Addition of some Excellent Poems, to those precedent, of Renowned *Shakespeare,* By other Gentlemen." This section consists of fifteen poems that have nothing to do with Shakespeare, most of them unattributed, a few signed with initials. They were written by Milton, Jonson, Beaumont, Herrick, Cartwright, Carew, Strode, and unidentified poets. Of Shakespeare's known poems, Benson's collection omits eight sonnets, *Venus and Adonis,* and *The Rape of Lucrece.*

The amount of Shakespeare's nondramatic verse preserved in these various publications is considerable —actually more than we have for some of the most widely admired lyric poets of the time. And some of this verse, such as the best of the sonnets, is very fine indeed, deserving a place with the best of Elizabethan poetry. But though the amount of his nondramatic verse is greater than one usually remembers, it is small in comparison with his plays, totaling less than the number of lines in two average-length plays; and though the quality of much of it is high, it does not tower above the achievements of other poets, as Shakespeare's greatest plays dominate the drama. A lyric and narrative poet of distinction he certainly was, but his incomparably greater achievement as a dramatist easily explains, though it does not justify, the popular image of Shakespeare's work as wholly dramatic.

CHAPTER 7

Shakespeare and the Printers

THE accounts of *The Passionate Pilgrim* and of
Shakespeare's *Sonnets* in the last chapter demonstrate
the fact that nondramatic writers had comparatively
little control over the publication of their works in the
reigns of Queen Elizabeth and James I. Dramatists had
even less.

To understand the circumstances of play publication
for William Shakespeare and his contemporaries, one
must keep in mind a fundamental fact: our idea of an
author's copyright in his play was not then widely or
legally acknowledged. If a printer got possession of a
play or a poem, there was no legal requirement at all
that he should get the permission of the author in
order to print it, or that he should consult the author
about the printing, or that he should pay him anything
at any time. The publisher was expected to meet the
requirements of the national censorship and of the
Stationers' Company of London, but that was all: there

were no requirements concerning his obligations to the author. Often publishers did pay authors for their work, and many times authors cooperated with publishers by writing prefaces or dedications and by reading proof in the printing shop, as Shakespeare appears to have done when Richard Field printed his *Venus and Adonis* and *The Rape of Lucrece;* but consideration for the writer was a matter of the kindness or the convenience or the sense of responsibility of the publisher, not of the author's legal rights. The concept that an author had a property right in what he had written did not achieve general acceptance and, ultimately, legal sanction until the reign of Queen Anne, 100 years after Shakespeare's time, when Parliament enacted a statute on the subject.

Failure to understand this fairly simple but unfamiliar and therefore difficult situation confuses most modern readers; it even confused most of the competent students of Shakespeare's texts and elicited frequent outbursts of indignation against "piratical Elizabethan publishers" until well into the twentieth century. It is hard to realize that when William Jaggard in 1599 published in *The Passionate Pilgrim* five poems of Shakespeare's without the author's cooperation or consent, he violated no legal right of Shakespeare, and the poet could have taken no legal steps to stop him. The publisher of *Love's Labour's Lost,* from which three of the poems had been taken, might have obtained some redress through the Stationers' Company, but not Shakespeare.

English printing and publishing in the late sixteenth and early seventeenth centuries was a closely held monopoly. In order to prevent the circulation of books and pamphlets that it considered to be unfavorable propaganda, the Tudor government eventually restricted all printing and publishing in the kingdom (except for that done by two or three privileged printers in Oxford and Cambridge) to the members of the Stationers' Company in London. This company was the guild of printers, publishers, and booksellers, and it exercised over its members a power that would now be thought tyrannical, regulating all their activities and punishing infringements with fines, confiscation of books, disabling and destruction of printing presses, and even imprisonment of the offending member. Such judicial and penal powers in the hands of the Court of the Stationers' Company were sanctioned by the Elizabethan government because the Master and Wardens of the company really policed the printing trades for Queen Elizabeth and her ministers, suppressing surreptitious printing, identifying the printers of objectionable books, and helping to keep seditious manuscripts out of print, as well as fostering what the leading printers thought to be their own best interests by restricting the number of printing presses, limiting the number of apprentices, holding down the number of copies that might be printed from one setting of type, and preventing price wars.

The Stationers' Company was obviously a very important factor in the publication of books in the time, and its importance is well illustrated by the ordinary procedure of an Elizabethan publisher when he got possession, by whatever means, of a manuscript that he thought he could print and sell at a profit. First he made sure that the government would have no objection to the appearance of the manuscript in print. The officials who could certify the manuscript were the Archbishop of Canterbury, the Bishop of London, the Lord Chamberlain, and other members of the Privy Council of the realm, but in most cases the work was too insignificant to take the time of such important officials, and it was examined by one of a panel of a dozen London clergymen named by the Archbishop. If this "corrector of the press" agreed that the manuscript seemed inoffensive, the publisher then took it to the headquarters of his guild, Stationers' Hall, on Paternoster Row behind St. Paul's Cathedral in London.

At Stationers' Hall one or both of the wardens (roughly first and second vice-presidents of the guild) inspected the manuscript to see that it had been duly approved, ascertained that no other member of the Company had registered his rights to it, and then certified that the publisher could have it printed and sold. The publisher then took his manuscript and the allowances of the corrector for the press and of the Wardens of the Stationers' Company to the clerk of the Company for entry in the Stationers' Register, an official record book of the Company. Most of the Registers may still be seen at Stationers' Hall. A typical entry is:

> 20 Octobr [1597]
> Andrewe wise / Entred for his copie vnder thand[es] of m^r Barlowe, and m^r warden man. / The tragedie of kinge Richard the Third with the death of the duke of Clarence   vj^d

Such an entry is the Company's official record of the facts (1) that Andrew Wise, a printer and publisher and a member in good standing of the Stationers' Company, brought in a manuscript of Shakespeare's play *Richard III* and asserted that the manuscript was his property; (2) that this manuscript had been certified as inoffensive by William Barlowe, one of the regular correctors for the press (Wise had been rather heavily fined by the Company two years before when he had published a book without this authorization); (3) that Thomas Man, one of the two Wardens of the Stationers'

Company for the year 1597, had inspected the manuscript and agreed that the allowance was in order and that Andrew Wise seemed to own it; and (4) that Andrew Wise had paid the Company's regular fee of sixpence to have the manuscript of *Richard III* recorded in the official book as his property so that no other printer could publish it without first making and recording satisfactory arrangements with him. It was this last provision that constituted the greatest importance of entry in the Stationers' Register. If, after Wise had published the play, any other printer brought out an edition of it without having Wise's consent explicitly recorded in the Register, Wise could show his original entry and the other publisher could be called before the Court of the Stationers' Company and punished; he might be fined, or the copies he had printed might be confiscated. Insofar as there was, in the time, any copyright (i.e. proof of legal ownership in right of copy), this was it—a protection of one publisher against the raids of another on his stock; the author had nothing to do with it. And an offended publisher who thought that some other printer had infringed his copyright appealed not to the courts of law but to the Court of the Stationers' Company.

During Shakespeare's lifetime there are entries in the Stationers' Register, like that of Andrew Wise for *Richard III,* for about half the dramatist's plays. Only three of these entries even mention the fact that Shakespeare was the author of the play entered, and none of the subsequent editions issued by the publishers who had made the entries shows the freedom from obvious errors of a text proofread by the author—the freedom from error found in *Venus and Adonis* and *The Rape of Lucrece.*

The conditions of Elizabethan publishing so far outlined applied with much the same force to the printing of any kind of literary manuscript, but for the dramatist there was still another condition of his relation to his manuscript that made him even more remote than other authors from the printed text of his composition. Playwrights prepared their manuscripts in the first instance not for readers—the market of the publishers—but for *actors,* who in turn prepared them for *audiences.* The playwright's sale of his manuscript to an acting company was thought to transfer all his moral rights (as we have seen, he had no *legal* rights to his copy before the law of 1709) to the actors, who could thereafter do with his manuscript what they pleased, and they generally thought it was to their advantage to keep the play out of print. In this belief the acting companies were undoubtedly correct, for once the play was in print, competing companies could buy copies for sixpence apiece and produce the play themselves, since there was no more copyright for a company than for an author. Accordingly the actors of each company, in order to keep the plays of its repertory exclusive to their own theater, tried to keep all its successful plays out of print.

In spite of the efforts of the companies that owned them, however, plays did get printed. In the years of Shakespeare's maturity—1586–1616—there were published and set out for sale in the London book shops about 180 plays from the repertories of London companies, in addition to about 80 masques, entertainments, pageants, translations, closet plays, and college plays in which professional acting troupes were not interested. Even though the 180 plays published from the professional repertories probably constitute not more than 15 to 20 per cent of those acted in London between the years 1586 and 1616, they still represent a large number to have escaped from the repertories of the acting companies. The explanation for the publication of many of them was superannuation, for others it was financial necessity. When a play could no longer draw audiences in a theater, the actors lost their interest in keeping it away from other companies, and it was profitable to realize a little cash by selling the manuscript to a publisher. When companies went bankrupt —a common phenomenon in the theater of any time— or were suppressed, something could be salvaged from the wreck by the sale of plays to the printers. In 1607 and 1608 many plays of the children's company called Paul's Boys were entered in the Stationers' Register, a circumstance explained by the fact that Paul's Boys had ceased to function as a London company at that time.

In many other instances actors were forced by hard times to sell manuscripts they would have preferred to keep exclusive. During the plague years of 1593 and 1594—the period of enforced idleness in the theaters that gave Shakespeare time to write *Venus and Adonis* and *The Rape of Lucrece*—more than a score of the plays of the London companies were published, though in the previous two years only eight of the plays of the professionals had got into print and in the following two-year period only five.

In a few instances manuscripts appear to have been stolen from the acting companies and sold to the printers. Sometimes abnormally inaccurate and abbreviated versions of plays reached publishers and were printed by them, resulting in what are now generally called "Bad Quartos." The origin of these mutilated texts is still a matter of some uncertainty, but it is conjectured that some of them were pieced together from memory, either by actors who were betraying the interests of their company or by touring actors on the road who did not have or could not use the full text of the play as it was written. Such versions were probably what

Shakespeare's friends and fellow sharers, John Heminges and Henry Condell, were referring to in their address to the readers of the First Folio when they spoke of some of the early quartos of his plays as

> stolne, and surreptitious copies, maimed, and deformed by the frauds and stealthes of iniurious impostors, that expos'd them.

Thomas Heywood, like Shakespeare an actor-dramatist, and a principal playwright for Queen Anne's company, had suffered a similar mutilation of some of his plays. In an address to the reader that he wrote for an edition of one of his plays in 1608 he recorded his experience and incidentally displayed the proper attitude of a regular playwright toward his responsibilities to his company:

> It hath beene no custome in mee . . . to commit my plaies to the presse: the reason, though some may attribute [it] to my own insufficiencie, [is that] I had rather subscribe in that to their seueare censure, then by seeking to auoide the imputation of weakenes, to incurre a greater suspition of honestie: for though some haue vsed a double sale of their labours, first to the Stage [i.e. to an acting company], and after to the presse, For my owne part I heere proclaime my selfe euer faithfull in the first, and neuer guiltie of the last: yet since some of my plaies haue (vnknown to me, and without any of my direction) accidentally come into the Printers handes, and therefore so corrupt and mangled, (coppied onely by the eare) that I haue bene as vnable to know them, as ashamde to chalenge them. This [play] therefore I was the willinger to furnish out in his natiue habit: first beeing

167

by consent [of the acting company], next because the rest haue beene so wronged in beeing publisht in such sauadge and ragged ornaments. . . .

All the circumstances so far noted through which plays written for the acting companies and owned by them got from their hands into the hands of the printers have one common feature: none of them involves the author of the play. One can generalize that the great majority of the plays published in England during Shakespeare's lifetime were clearly not seen through the press by the author and probably not brought to the publisher by him. Apparently most playwrights felt as Heywood did, that "honestie" would not allow them to make "a double sale of their labours, first to the Stage, and after to the presse."

There are, however, a certain number of exceptional plays published between 1586 and 1616 that do show evidence of some degree of consent or cooperation by their authors with the publishers. About half of these sponsored publications had been written for the children's companies, whose playwrights appear always to have retained an unusual amount of control over their writings. There still remain about twenty out of the 180 published plays that show evidence of an author's cooperation with the publisher—plays written for and owned by the regular adult companies, such as the Lord Chamberlain–King's men, the Lord Admiral–Prince Henry's men, and the Earl of Worcester–Queen Anne's men, and exceptions to the general rule that in Shakespeare's lifetime dramatists did not cooperate with printers in the publication of their plays. Several of them are plays that got to the publishers without the author's cooperation or consent but for which, upon learning that his play was about to come out, the author cooperated so far as to write an address to the reader, as Heywood did for his *Golden Age* in 1611 and for his *Four Prentices of London* in 1615.

As noted above (pp. 100–1), the one dramatist who was consistently eccentric to the Elizabethan pattern of playwright indifference to the printed texts of their plays was Ben Jonson, and the distinction of his plays and the influence of his name often confuse modern readers who do not realize the abnormality of his practice. When Jonson wrote addresses and dedications for his plays and collected commendatory verses for them, when he carefully revised the texts and scrupulously read proof, he was treating his plays as many twentieth-century playwrights have treated theirs, and consequently his conduct seems normal to us. In his time, however, he was unique; no one else dealt with play texts in this fashion, and various of his contemporaries laughed at him for taking his own so seriously. Shakespeare's indifference to his plays outside the medium of the theater for which they were written is the normal attitude of the time; Jonson, who treated his plays in what may seem a normal fashion, displayed the abnormality. Indeed, more than two hundred years elapsed before any other English playwright prepared his plays for posterity as carefully as Ben Jonson did.

The fact that Shakespeare took no active part in the process of getting his plays before the reading public is abundantly clear in the early texts of these works. In the first place, slightly more than half his dramatic work had never been printed by the time of his death. Of the eighteen of his plays that were published in quarto during his lifetime, none shows any of those ordinary helps for the reader that we now take for granted. All the Shakespeare quartos lack most of the stage directions so important in helping readers imagine what actors are doing as they speak the lines. None has a list of characters or dramatis personae; none has any separate indication of the general locality of the action; none has any division into acts and scenes.

In fact these quartos come naked into the world. They do not have any preface or address to the reader, or a dedication to an influential patron; they are not commended to the reader by laudatory verses provided by the author's friends. The front matter of three-fourths of the quartos published before 1616 consists barely and sparely of a title page with the name of the play, the publisher's imprint, usually the name of the acting company, and only about half the time the name of the author. Following the title on the next page is the head title, under which comes the first entrance; the dialogue commences at once and continues straight on to the end of the play without any break or any orienting aid to the reader.

Several of the quartos show minor variations from this formula, but the variations are not the result of the author's care. Two quartos, *Henry IV, Part 2*, 1600, and *Pericles*, 1609, have prologues and epilogues; the three quartos of *Romeo and Juliet* print a prologue for the play, and in the first *Romeo and Juliet* quarto of 1597 the text is broken here and there by a series of type ornaments across the page. These ornaments might be thought to indicate scene breaks, but several of them occur in the middle of scenes and they are found in only the last two-thirds of the play. One of the two issues of *Troilus and Cressida* printed in 1609 has an epistle to the reader, but it was written not by the author, as Jonson's and Heywood's were, but by the publisher as a device to sell his book, like the blurbs on the dust jackets of modern novels.

Besides these omissions, which in themselves make an original quarto edition of a Shakespeare play very difficult for the uninitiated to read, all the quartos show errors too obvious to have escaped the eye of a proofreading author. The following examples are not particularly unusual ones.

In the trial scene in *The Merchant of Venice,* when Antonio persuades Bassanio that it is useless to reason with Shylock, we are accustomed to read:

> You may as well go stand upon the beach,
> And bid the main flood bate his usual height;
> You may as well use question with the wolf,
> Why he hath made the ewe bleat for the lamb.

But in *The Merchant of Venice* quarto of 1600 the lines are:

> you may as well goe stand vpon the Beach
> and bid the maine flood bate his vsuall height,
> well vse question with the Woolfe,
> the Ewe bleake for the Lambe.

In the third act of *Hamlet,* the Prince comes unexpectedly upon the King at his prayers. Hamlet starts to accomplish his revenge, then stops to reason himself out of it, saying:

> A villain kills my father, and for that,
> I, his sole son, do this same villain send
> To heaven.
> Why, this is hire and salary, not revenge.

The 1604 quarto of the play—the Good Quarto—makes the last line of this passage read

> Why, this is base and silly, not reuendge

Act III, Scene 2 of *King Richard III* opens with the entrance of a messenger who has come to Lord Hastings from Lord Stanley to tell of an ominous dream Stanley has had about the bloody and ambitious Richard, whose heraldic insignia was the wild boar. In modern editions Lord Stanley's emissary delivers this message:

> Then certifies your lordship, that this night
> He dreamt the boar had rased off his helm.

In the quarto of 1597 the baldly paraphrased passage loses all its significance by naming an heraldic animal that would not suggest the tyrant Richard at all:

> And then he sends you word.
> He dreamt to night the beare had raste his helme.

In Act IV, Scene 6 of *King Lear* the distrait king moralizes to Gloucester over the sad state of the world:

> LEAR. . . . . Thou hast seen a farmer's dog bark at a beggar?
>
> GLOUCESTER. Ay, sir.
>
> LEAR. And the creature run from the cur? There thou mightst behold the great image of authority: a dog's obey'd in office.

In the quarto of 1608 Lear's line reads,

> . . . there thou mightst behold the great image of authoritie, a dogge, so bade in office.

These passages—and there are many similar ones—so pervert the meaning that no author could have read them in proof and failed to see that correction was needed. The multiplicity of such errors is sufficient to make it clear that none of the quarto editions of his plays appearing in his lifetime could have been proof-read by Shakespeare. Of these quarto editions before 1616 there is a good number, and they vary widely in character. The plays issued for sale in London before Shakespeare's death are as follows:

1594 The Most Lamentable Romaine Tragedie of
Titus Andronicus: As it was Plaide by the
Right Honourable the Earle of Darbie, Earle
of Pembrooke, and Earle of Sussex their
Seruants. . . . 1594.

This play was reprinted in a second quarto in 1600
and in a third in 1611. The third quarto changes the
statement about the producing company to "As It Hath
Svndry times beene plaide by the Kings Maiesties Seruants," but none of the quartos names any author on
the title page.

1594 The First part of the Contention betwixt the
two famous Houses of Yorke and Lancaster,
with the death of the good Duke Humphrey:
And the banishment and death of the Duke
of Suffolke, and the Tragicall end of the
proud Cardinall of Winchester, with the
notable Rebellion of Iacke Cade: And the
Duke of Yorkes first claime vnto the Crowne.
. . . 1594.

This play was reprinted in a second quarto of 1600,
also without any author's name on the title page. It is
a version of Shakespeare's *Henry VI, Part 2,* but it is
only about two-thirds the length of that play, and there
are hundreds of differences in phrasing, vocabulary,
order, meter, so that scarcely 10 per cent of the lines
in the Folio of 1623 are identical with those in the
quarto. Indeed the differences are so great that it was
long thought that *The First Part of the Contention* was
written by some other writer and that Shakespeare
merely revised it into the *Henry VI, Part 2* of the Folio. Fuller study in the twentieth century has convinced
most scholars that *Henry VI, Part 2* is the original and
that *The First Part of the Contention* was printed from

a manuscript hastily and probably fraudulently assembled by parties unknown who had a fairly good but imperfect knowledge of *Henry VI, Part 2.* In other words, it is a "Bad Quarto."

> 1594 A Pleasant Conceited Historie, called The taming of a Shrew. As it was sundry times acted by the Right honorable the Earle of Pembrook his seruants. . . . 1594.

This play, which was reprinted in a second quarto in 1596 and a third in 1607, all without any author's name, is related to *The Taming of the Shrew* in the Folio of 1623 somewhat as *The First Part of the Contention* is related to *Henry VI, Part 2,* except that the differences, including the names of all but one of the characters, are greater. So much greater, in fact, that most scholars think that in this case *The Taming of a Shrew* is really not by Shakespeare but by another whose work he revised into *The Taming of the Shrew.* If the majority is right, *The Taming of a Shrew* does not belong among the Shakespeare quartos; if the minority is right, it is another very Bad Quarto.

> 1595 The true Tragedie of Richard Duke of Yorke, and the death of good King Henrie the Sixt, with the whole contention betweene the two Houses Lancaster and Yorke, as it was sundrie times acted by the Right Honourable the Earle of Pembrooke his seruants. . . . 1595.

The True Tragedy, an octavo which was reprinted as a quarto in 1600, is related to *Henry VI, Part 3* of the Folio much as *The First Part of the Contention* is related to *Henry VI, Part 2,* except that it is about three-fourths instead of only two-thirds the length, and more of its lines correspond approximately to those

of the Folio. Scholars long thought it to be a play by
unknown dramatists which Shakespeare revised into
Henry VI, Part 3, but now most of them agree that it
seems more likely to be an extremely inaccurate version
of Shakespeare's play, probably printed from a manuscript hastily assembled by someone whose memory
of Shakespeare's play was very good but not precise or
complete.

> 1597 The Tragedie of King Richard the second.
> As it hath beene publikely acted by the right
> Honourable the Lorde Chamberlaine his
> Seruants. . . . 1597.

Richard II was one of Shakespeare's more popular
plays, and before his death it had been four times reprinted: twice in 1598, once in 1608, and again in 1615.
The quarto of 1597 is one of the more accurate of the
quarto texts, but there is still an average of one word
wrong per page, the punctuation is inadequate, and
some of the lines have been run together. In the three
quartos of *Richard II* published before the death of
Queen Elizabeth, lines 154–318 of Act IV, Scene 1, the
deposition scene, are always omitted.

> 1597 The Tragedy Of King Richard the third.
> Containing, His treacherous Plots against
> his brother Clarence: the pittiefull murther
> of his innocent nephewes: his tyrannicall
> vsurpation: with the whole course of his de-
> tested life, and most deserued death. As it
> hath beene lately Acted by the Right hon-
> ourable the Lord Chamberlaine his seruants.
> . . . 1597.

Richard III was even more popular with readers than
Richard II, for it was not only reprinted four times
before Shakespeare's death, in 1598, 1602, 1605, and

1612, but in addition to the printings in the four folios it was also issued in later editions of 1622, 1629, and 1634. The first quarto is less good than that of *Richard II;* as compared with the text of the play in the Folio, more than 200 lines, representing passages of one to seventeen lines in length, have been cut, or perhaps inadvertently omitted; many words are changed, though usually without serious alteration of the sense; and many of the stage directions are shorter.

> 1597 An Excellent conceited Tragedie of Romeo
> and Iuliet. As it hath been often (with great
> applause) plaid publiquely, by the right
> Honourable the L. of Hunsdon his Seruants.
> . . . 1597.

This edition of Shakespeare's tragedy is another of that group of plays so garbled in the printing that they are commonly called the Bad Quartos. It omits one-fourth of the lines found in all good modern editions; sometimes the lines and phrases are out of order; in places the action is only described and most of the lines are omitted. A much better version was published in the quarto of 1599 and reprinted in 1609 and in a fourth undated quarto printed later, perhaps after Shakespeare's death.

> 1598 The History Of Henrie the Fovrth; With the
> battell at Shrewsburie, betweene the King
> and Lord Henry Percy, surnamed Henrie
> Hotspur of the North. With the humorous
> conceits of Sir Iohn Falstalffe. . . . 1598.

This quarto is one of the better ones. It seems to have been preceded by an earlier quarto of which only a fragment of one copy has been preserved—one sheet, which had been used in the binding of another book. Later quartos were printed in 1599, 1604, 1608, and

1613, and after Shakespeare's death there were, in addition to the four folios, editions in 1622, 1632, and 1639, making it the Shakespearean play most frequently reprinted before the Restoration.

> 1598 A Pleasant Conceited Comedie Called, Loues labors lost. As it was presented before her Highnes this last Christmas. Newly corrected and augmented By W. Shakespere. . . . 1598.

The words "Newly corrected and augmented By W. Shakespere" imply that there had been an earlier edition of this comedy, but no copy of an earlier edition is known to exist, and it may be that the words are only a publisher's come-on. No later quarto appeared until 1631. The title page of *Love's Labor's Lost,* 1598, is the first exhibition of Shakespeare's name before a new play, though it had appeared after the dedications of *Venus and Adonis* in 1593 and of *The Rape of Lucrece* in 1594, and in this same year, 1598, the *second* editions of *Richard II* and *Richard III* carried it. The notable fact is that the first eight plays of Shakespeare to appear in print did not seem to their publishers apt to derive any advantage from the display of his name. Later some of these same publishers changed their minds, and after 1598 it was usual, though not invariable, for publishers to print Shakespeare's name on the title pages of his plays. The advertising zeal of some even went so far as to put his name on the title pages of plays he did not write, like *The London Prodigal,* 1605, *A Yorkshire Tragedy,* 1608, and *Sir John Oldcastle,* 1619 (falsely dated 1600).

> 1600 The Cronicle History of Henry the fift, With his battell fought at Agin Court in France. Togither with Auntient Pistoll. As it hath

bene sundry times playd by the Right honorable the Lord Chamberlaine his seruants. . . . 1600.

The first edition of *Henry V* is another of the Bad Quartos. It leaves out almost half the lines published in the Folio of 1623: whole scenes are omitted, some scenes are out of order, characters are left out, the prologue, epilogue, and choruses are omitted, and in what does appear lines are paraphrased and much of the verse is spoiled, though without radically altering the sense. This Bad Quarto was reprinted in 1602 and in 1619 with only minor variations. The edition of 1619 is dated 1608, as part of a publisher's fraud involving several other plays.

> 1600 The Second part of Henrie the fourth, continuing to his death, and coronation of Henrie the fift. With the humours of sir Iohn Falstaffe, and swaggering Pistoll. As it hath been sundrie times publikely acted by the right honourable, the Lord Chamberlaine his seruants. Written by William Shakespeare. . . . 1600.

This is the only edition of the play during Shakespeare's lifetime, but there are two different issues: when the play was first printed, Act III, Scene 1 was omitted, and the play was reissued in the same year with two leaves canceled and four new ones substituted to get in the missing scene. Eight Folio passages of from three to thirty-six lines each are missing from the quarto; the names given in some of the stage directions do not agree with the names of the characters speaking the lines, and once an actor's name instead of that of a character is used.

1600 Much adoe about Nothing. As it hath been
sundrie times publikely acted by the right
honourable, the Lord Chamberlaine his seruants. Written by William Shakespeare. . . .
1600.

Much Ado about Nothing was printed only once in
Shakespeare's lifetime and thereafter only in the four
folios before the end of the century. The quarto omits
a number of necessary entrances and exits; there is confusion in the names of a number of the characters—for
example, Dogberry and Verges are variously designated, a few times by the names of the actors, Kempe
and Cowley, who played the parts; entrances but no
speeches are given to characters like "Innogen," Leon-
ato's wife.

1600 A Midsommer nights dreame. As it hath
beene sundry times publickely acted, by the
Right honourable, the Lord Chamberlaine
his seruants. Written by William Shakespeare. . . . 1600.

This is the only edition of the play to appear in
Shakespeare's lifetime, though three years after his
death a reprint appeared that was fraudulently dated
1600. There is reason for thinking that the text of the
first quarto was revised somewhat before the play was
printed in the Folio; it perhaps represents alterations
for a later production.

1600 The most excellent Historie of the Merchant
of Venice. With the extreame crueltie of Shy-
locke the Iewe towards the sayd Merchant,
in cutting a iust pound of his flesh: and the
obtayning of Portia by the choyse of three
chests. As it hath beene diuers times acted
by the Lord Chamberlaine his Seruants.
Written by William Shakespeare. . . . 1600.

The Merchant of Venice, like *A Midsummer Night's Dream,* and *King Lear,* was printed only once in Shakespeare's lifetime, but in 1619 these three with several other plays were reprinted without changes, with the dates of the original quartos fraudulently printed on their title pages. The fraud caused much confusion among Shakespeare's editors until it was detected and explained by A. W. Pollard and W. W. Greg. The genuine 1600 edition of *The Merchant of Venice* is better printed than many of the quartos, but even so there are numerous errors in punctuation, capitalization, and lineation, and several exits and an entrance are omitted.

> 1602 A Most pleasaunt and excellent conceited Comedie, of Syr Iohn Falstaffe, and the merrie Wiues of Windsor. Entermixed with sundrie variable and pleasing humors, of Syr Hugh the Welch Knight, Iustice Shallow, and his wise Cousin M. Slender. With the swaggering vaine of Auncient Pistoll, and Corporall Nym. By William Shakespeare. As it hath bene diuers times Acted by the right Honorable my Lord Chamberlaines seruants. Both before her Maiestie, and else-where. . . . 1602.

The 1602 edition of *The Merry Wives of Windsor* is the only one printed before Shakespeare's death, though there is a fraudulent reprint of 1619. The real 1602 edition is another of the Bad Quartos. Five scenes familiar in modern editions (all derived from the Folio of 1623) are omitted altogether; two other scenes and many short passages are out of order; hundreds of lines are omitted, so that the quarto play is only a little more than half the length of the version in the Folio. Even the lines that approximate each other in the two versions are often so different in wording that they merely convey a similar, not an identical sense, as when Slender boasts to Anne of his familiarity with the bears, saying in the Folio, "I haue seene *Sackerson* loose, twenty times, and haue taken him by the Chaine," and in the quarto, "Ile run yon to a Beare, and take her by the mussell, You neuer saw the like."

> 1603 The Tragicall Historie of Hamlet Prince of Denmarke. By William Shake-speare. As it hath beene diuerse times acted by his Highnesse seruants in the Cittie of London: as also in the two Vniuersities of Cambridge and Oxford, and else-where. . . 1603.

The first edition of *Hamlet* is another Bad Quarto, but for this popular play a completely different version, a Good Quarto, appeared in 1604, and it was reprinted in 1611 and again at an unknown date, probably after Shakespeare's death. The quarto of 1603 differs in numerous and complex ways from the Good Quarto and the Folio. It is only a little more than half their length; some characters are called by different names: Polonius is Corambis, Reynaldo is Montano, Osric is a Braggart Gentleman; scenes are omitted or reordered; many passages are summaries or approximations of similar ones in the second quarto and the Folio. The differences between the quarto of 1603 and the 1604 quarto and the Folio are, in fact, so many and so various that there is still uncertainty as to what the early version represents.

> 1608 M. William Shak-speare: His True Chronicle Historie of the life and death of King Lear and his three Daughters. With the vnfortunate life of Edgar, sonne and heire to the Earle of Gloster, and his sullen and assumed humor of Tom of Bedlam: As it was played

181

> before the Kings Maiestie at Whitehall vpon
> S. Stephans night in Christmas Hollidayes.
> By his Maiesties seruants playing vsually at
> the Gloabe on the Bancke-side. . . . 1608.

The 1608 quarto of *King Lear,* sometimes called the "Pied Bull" quarto from the name of the shop in which it was to be sold, was not reprinted in Shakespeare's lifetime, though another edition that was printed in 1619 was fraudulently dated 1608. The "Pied Bull" quarto is not so bad as the truly Bad Quartos nor so good as most of the good ones. Many prose lines are printed as verse and verse lines as prose, punctuation is confusing, a number of lines are omitted, and others are unintelligible. For instance, when Goneril speaks to her husband of the French invasion of England, she says,

> *France* spreds his banners in our noyseles land
> With plumed helme, thy state begins thereat.

And at the end of his soliloquy beginning the second scene Edmund, in resolving to supersede his legitimate brother, says,

> Well my legitimate, if this letter speede, and my
> inuention thriue, *Edmund* the base shall tooth'
> legitimate.

> 1609 The Historie of Troylus and Cresseida. As
> it was acted by the Kings Maiesties seruants
> at the Globe. Written by William Shake-
> speare. . . . 1609.

Two issues of this quarto appeared in 1609; for the second, the statement about performance was removed from the title page and there was added an address to the reader claiming that the play was "neuer stal'd with the Stage, neuer clapper-clawd with the palmes of the vulger . . . not . . . sullied, with the smoaky breath of the multitude." The implication that the play had never been acted at all is scarcely credible; the publisher may mean that it was never acted in a public theater—and he may be mistaken. Both issues omit a number of passages found in the Folio.

> 1609 The Late, And much admired Play, Called Pericles, Prince of Tyre. With the true Relation of the whole Historie, aduentures, and fortunes of the said Prince: As also, The no lesse strange, and worthy accidents, in the Birth and Life, of his Daughter Mariana. As it hath been diuers and sundry times acted by his Maiesties Seruants, at the Globe on the Banck-side. By William Shakespeare. . . . 1609.

Before Shakespeare's death *Pericles* was printed in a second quarto of 1609 and a third of 1611, but it was not included in the Folio of 1623. This omission, taken with the apparently un-Shakespearean writing of parts of the play, has led most critics to say that, in spite of the title page, *Pericles* is only partly Shakespeare's work. In any case, the quarto is full of errors that often render verse as prose and make nonsense of many speeches.

These nineteen plays (one of which, *The Taming of a Shrew,* is probably not his work) are the only ones of Shakespeare's dramatic compositions, or partial compositions, that he could ever have seen in print. Not one of them was printed just as he had written it, and four of them—*Henry VI, Part 2, Henry VI, Part 3, Henry V,* and *The Merry Wives of Windsor*—were so distorted in all the editions printed during his lifetime that, if he saw them, he must have found them either ludicrous or horrifying. Whether he ever looked at them or collected copies of them no one knows, but it is obvious that he did nothing about seeing them through the press to ensure that posterity would receive accurate transcripts of what he had written. Posterity has often found this neglect incredible. Actually it is simply another of the many pieces of evidence that Shakespeare was primarily a man of the theater; his act of creation reached its fulfillment when his actors presented his play before an audience.

The preservation of his plays for posterity—including the first printing of eighteen of them—was accomplished by two of Shakespeare's longtime friends and associates in the theater, John Heminges and Henry Condell, the leaders of the King's company at the time. Both these men had been fellow sharers of the Lord Chamberlain–King's company and house-keepers at the Globe and Blackfriars for as long a time as Shakespeare had been; both were remembered by Shakespeare in his will; and both continued as leading members of the acting company for years after his death. The collected edition they sponsored was very much a memorial to an actor-dramatist by his actor friends. The handsome folio volume was entitled

> Mr. William Shakespeares Comedies, Histories, & Tragedies. Published according to the True Originall Copies.

It bore on the title page a large engraving of Shakespeare—the only well-authenticated portrait of the dramatist known to exist. Following the title page comes Heminges' and Condell's dedication of their volume to two members of the Herbert family, William, Earl of Pembroke, and his brother Philip, Earl of Montgomery. Both these noblemen had been friends of the actors and admirers of the plays, for the two leaders of the King's company in their dedication speak

of their gratitude "for the many fauors we haue receiued from your [Lordships]" and note that their
Lordships

> haue beene pleas'd to thinke these trifles some-
> thing, heeretofore; and haue prosequuted both
> them, and their Authour liuing, with so much fa-
> uour . . . For, so much were your [Lordships'] lik-
> ings of the seuerall parts, when they were acted, as
> before they were published, the Volume ask'd to
> be yours. We haue but collected them, and done an
> office to the dead, to procure his Orphanes, Guard-
> ians; without ambition either of selfe-profit, or
> fame: onely to keepe the memory of so so worthy a
> Freind, & Fellow aliue, as was our *Shakespeare,* by
> humble offer of his playes, to your most noble
> patronage.

The reference to Shakespeare as their "Freind, &
Fellow" shows Heminges and Condell thinking of the
dramatist not primarily as a great writer but as their
friend and colleague, a "Fellow" of the King's company, the most distinguished and prosperous troupe of
actors in London. The very selection of the Earl of
Pembroke as a patron for the volume is an actor's selection, for the Earl held the office of Lord Chamberlain at the time, and the Lord Chamberlain, as the im-
mediate superior of the Master of the Revels (who in
1622–23 was still a third member of the Herbert family) was the final arbiter of the destinies of actors, dramatists, and theater owners. Indeed, the unspecified
"many fauors we haue receiued" mentioned in the
dedication were very likely favors which Pembroke, as
Lord Chamberlain, had done for the company. One
such had occurred not long before, in May 1619, when
Pembroke in his official capacity had written to the
Stationers' Company of London ordering that no Lon-

don publisher should print any play belonging to the King's company without the express permission of the representatives of the company. At that time the regular representatives had been John Heminges and Henry Condell. Such a large extralegal favor from the Lord Chamberlain certainly merited the gratitude expressed by Heminges and Condell in their dedication to him.

Pembroke had also a personal feeling for at least one other fellow of Heminges, Condell, and Shakespeare in the King's company, for shortly after the death in March 1619 of Richard Burbage, the greatest actor of the company and one of the three actor-friends of Shakespeare remembered in his will, Pembroke had written a letter to Lord Doncaster saying that he was sitting alone while the rest of the guests were attending the private performance of a play

> which I being tender-harted, could not endure to see so soone after the loss of my old acquaintance Burbage.

What connection Pembroke's brother, the Earl of Montgomery, had with the actors at this time is unknown, but that there probably was some may be guessed from the fact that three years later when the Earl of Pembroke resigned as Lord Chamberlain, he was succeeded in the office by the Earl of Montgomery, who was even more considerate of the King's company in his official acts than his brother had been. Heminges and Condell, then, in dedicating to Pembroke and Montgomery this collection of thirty-six of Shakespeare's plays—all part of the repertory of their company at the Globe and Blackfriars—had made a very shrewd actors' choice of patrons for the published plays of their "Freind, & Fellow."

Following the dedication in the Folio, Heminges and Condell inserted another foreword, an address *"To*

186

the great Variety of Readers." After urging readers
to buy the book, they continue:

> But, what euer you do, Buy. Censure will not
> driue a Trade, or make the Iacke go. And though
> you be a Magistrate of wit, and sit on the Stage at
> *Black-Friers,* or the *Cock-pit,* to arraigne Playes
> dailie, know, these Playes haue had their triall al-
> readie, and stood out all Appeales; and do now
> come forth quitted rather by a Decree of Court,
> then any purchas'd Letters of commendation.
>
> It had bene a thing, we confesse, worthie to
> haue bene wished, that the Author himselfe had
> liu'd to haue set forth, and ouerseen his owne
> writings; But since it hath bin ordain'd otherwise,
> and he by death departed from that right, we pray
> you do not envie his Friends, the office of their
> care, and paine, to haue collected & publish'd
> them; and so to haue publish'd them, as where
> (before) you were abus'd with diuerse stolne, and
> surreptitious copies, maimed, and deformed by the
> frauds and stealthes of iniurious impostors, that
> expos'd them: euen those, are now offer'd to your
> view cur'd, and perfect of their limbes; and all the
> rest, absolute in their numbers, as he conceiued
> thē.

The statement about previous editions of Shakespeare's plays which had been "stolne . . . maimed, and
deformed," issued by "iniurious impostors," was long
thought to refer to all the early quarto editions and
their publishers, but later investigations have shown
that the text printed in some of these quartos was as
good as or better than the corresponding one in the
Folio, and that several of the quarto publishers were
honest businessmen: one or two of them had repeatedly
been trusted by the company. Heminges and Condell

were apparently referring to the Bad Quartos—like the first editions of *Romeo and Juliet, Henry V, The Merry Wives of Windsor,* and *Hamlet*—and not to all quartos.

Even in this address to readers Heminges and Condell still tend to think of Shakespeare and his plays in a theatrical rather than a literary context. They recommend the plays because of their success on the stage, and they address specifically the superior members of the audience at the two most distinguished theaters in 1622–23, their own playhouse of Blackfriars and its principal competitor, the Cockpit or Phoenix in Drury Lane.

Following Heminges' and Condell's address to the readers in the Folio come two poems in praise of Shakespeare, a rather long one by Ben Jonson and a short one by Hugh Holland. The Jonson poem is one of the best-known tributes to Shakespeare; it calls him "The applause! delight! the wonder of our Stage!," admits that he had "small *Latine,* and lesse *Greeke*" but nevertheless compares him to Sophocles, Aeschylus, and Euripides, and exalts him with the famous sentence, "He was not of an age, but for all time!"

After these poems comes the table of contents, dividing the plays into three categories as the title page does—"Comedies, Histories, & Tragedies"—with each category separately paged as if the plays were to make up three volumes. Two more commendatory poems, one by Leonard Digges and one by "I.M.," probably James Mabbe, follow the table of contents. Finally, just before the text of the first play, comes a most unusual feature, one never found before in an English collection and seldom since. It is a list of actors, headed "The Names of the Principall Actors in all these Playes." Such a list placed conspicuously on a separate page at the beginning of the largest collection of plays hitherto printed in England is eloquent of the theatrical character of the volume and of Heminges' and Condell's presentation of these plays from the repertory of the King's company "onely to keepe the memory of so worthy a Freind, & Fellow aliue, as was our *Shakespeare*." The list of the twenty-six Lord Chamberlain–King's men begins appropriately with William Shakespeare, followed by the company's greatest actor, Richard Burbage, then John Heminges, later Henry Condell, and includes all the players who had been, like Shakespeare, Burbage, Heminges, and Condell, fellows or sharers in the troupe.

Immediately after "The Names of the Principall Actors in all these Playes" the dramatic texts begin: fourteen comedies, commencing with *The Tempest* and ending with *The Winter's Tale;* ten histories, beginning with *King John* and ending with *King Henry the Eighth;* and eleven tragedies, beginning with *Coriolanus* and ending with *Cymbeline,* the last wrongly classified. Between the histories and the tragedies in a belatedly inserted section, unpaged and omitted from the table of contents, comes *Troilus and Cressida.*

The plays that had previously appeared in good quarto editions generally read in the Folio much as they had in the last quarto edition, with minor additions, deletions, or alterations, and errors in copying; for a few plays a list of dramatis personae has been added, some have had act and scene divisions added, some act divisions only, and some still have neither. For those plays that had previously appeared in Bad Quartos only—2 and 3 *Henry VI, Henry V,* and *The Merry Wives of Windsor*—a completely new text was printed from papers available to the players.

The Folio prints eighteen plays that had never before been published: *Henry VI, Part 1, The Comedy of Errors, The Taming of the Shrew* (assuming that *The*

Taming of a Shrew of 1594 is not a Bad Quarto of Shakespeare's play, but his source), *The Two Gentlemen of Verona, King John, Julius Caesar, As You Like It, Twelfth Night, All's Well That Ends Well, Measure for Measure, Macbeth, Antony and Cleopatra, Coriolanus, Timon of Athens, Cymbeline, The Winter's Tale, The Tempest,* and *King Henry VIII. (Othello,* which was not printed in Shakespeare's lifetime, had appeared in a quarto after his death, but before the Folio, in 1622.) Members of the King's company must have brought to the printers from the archives of the Globe or Blackfriars the manuscripts for all or nearly all these eighteen plays—the prompt copy, or the author's own manuscript from which the prompt copy had been made, or some professional scribe's transcript.

The thirty-six plays printed in the First Folio constitute the most generally accepted canon of Shakespeare's dramatic work. There are, however, two plays in the Folio, *King Henry VIII* and *Timon of Athens,* which are often rejected in part, and there are three plays outside the Folio for which most scholars think that Shakespeare was partially responsible. The three plays that Heminges and Condell omitted from the First Folio are *Pericles, Prince of Tyre, Sir Thomas More,* and *The Two Noble Kinsmen.*

Pericles, Prince of Tyre was first printed in a quarto of 1609 whose title page bore the statement,

> As it hath been diuers and sundry times acted by his Maiesties Seruants, at the Globe on the Banckside. By William Shakespeare.

This quarto was printed a second time in 1609 and again in 1611, 1619, 1630, and 1635, always with Shakespeare's name on the title page. A majority of critics are inclined to think that *Pericles* was written by Shakespeare, at least in part, and it is included in most modern editions. The style of the writing in Acts I and II is quite different from that in Acts III, IV, and V, which resemble the style he used in his late romances, and many scholars have therefore concluded that Shakespeare wrote the last three acts only. There is much confusion in the text of the play, however, and it has been suggested that the marked differences between the two parts may be due to two different reporters rather than to two different authors.

Another omitted play, *Sir Thomas More,* was not printed until the nineteenth century. Before that time it existed only in a manuscript now preserved in the Harleian collection in the British Museum, a manuscript that has been censored by the Master of the Revels and much revised and worked over. Six different handwritings can be identified in it. One hand has written the entire original manuscript and made later revisions as well, but five other hands (designated A, B, C, D, and E) have also made additions and revisions. One of these five hands, that called D, is now thought by many scholars to be Shakespeare's. This hand has written one scene occupying three pages in the manuscript, in which Sir Thomas More quells a London riot. If one agrees that the handwriting is Shakespeare's and the composition his, the addition to the canon of his work is negligible; its importance lies in the fact that here we may have a sample of unrevised composition that shows how he wrote out the text of a play. His peculiarities of spelling, letter formation, abbreviation, capitalization, and punctuation and his methods of insertion and deletion, once established, will show the kinds of errors compositors and copyists could most easily have made in setting up or transcribing his manuscripts. The many hundreds of mistakes that compositors and copyists made because they misread the handwriting and that are, in many instances, still uncorrected, may eventually, through the analysis of the writing of Hand D in the messy manuscript of *Sir Thomas More,* be replaced by Shakespeare's true words.

The Two Noble Kinsmen, the last of the three plays omitted from the Folio, was not published until Shakespeare had been dead for eighteen years. It appeared with a title page that read:

> The Two Noble Kinsmen: Presented at the Blackfriers by the Kings Maiesties servants, with great applause: Written by the memorable Worthies of their time;
>
> (M^r. *John Fletcher,* and) Gent.
> (M^r. *William Shakspeare.*)
>
> . . . 1634

This title-page attribution has been generally, though not invariably, accepted as accurate by modern scholars. Borrowings and allusions indicate that the play was probably composed in 1613, and about this time Shakespeare was withdrawing from London theatrical activities for his Stratford retirement; in succession John Fletcher became the principal playwright of the King's company, for whom he composed at least thirty-five plays between 1613 and 1625. Collaboration in a new play between the retiring dramatist of the King's company and his successor seems likely enough. Critics who have analyzed the verse of *The Two Noble Kinsmen* have usually found many passages that they thought characteristic of Fletcher's distinctive style and other passages almost equally characteristic of Shakespeare in his last period. A few critics think the entire play is Shakespeare's. Why Heminges and Condell did not include *The Two Noble Kinsmen* in the Folio of 1623 is a puzzle.

There was once another play, now lost, in which Shakespeare and Fletcher are said to have collaborated.

On 20 May 1613 John Heminges was paid £153 6s. 8d.
for twenty plays (half a dozen of them by Shakespeare)
which the King's company had presented at court in
the course of the preceding winter. One of the plays
was called "Cardenno." Seven weeks later John Heminges was again paid for a play performed at court by
the company, this time before the Ambassador of the
Duke of Savoy on 8 June 1613; the play was called
"Cardenna." The author of the play is not named, and
it was never printed. But forty years later Humphrey
Moseley, the greatest dramatic publisher of his time,
had a manuscript that he intended to publish and that
he entered in the Stationers' Register on 9 September
1653 as

> The History of Cardennio,
> by M^r. Fletcher. & Shakespeare.

It is possible that one or more manuscripts of this
play were still in existence in the 1720's, for on 13
December 1727 a play by Lewis Theobald called *Double Falsehood* was performed at Drury Lane Theatre.
Theobald said that his play was an adaptation of a
manuscript play of Shakespeare. *Double Falsehood* is
a poor thing, but it is based on the story of Cardenio
and Lucinda in *Don Quixote,* though the names have
been changed. It is highly unlikely that Theobald
could have known of any of the three seventeenth-century records of the King's Men's *Cardenno.* Very few
of Theobald's contemporaries believed that he had a
manuscript of a play by Shakespeare; indeed he says
that some of them said that it came "nearer to the Style
and Manner of *Fletcher,*" a suggestion that Theobald
received with contempt. It is probably impossible now
to find out what the manuscript was that Theobald
had, but certainly in 1613 there was a play called
Cardenno, and it may be that it was a collaboration of

Shakespeare and Fletcher. If it was, the question again arises: Why did not Heminges and Condell include it in the First Folio?

As noted above, two of the plays that they did include, *The Famous History of the Life of King Henry the Eighth* and *The Life of Timon of Athens,* have often been thought to be not wholly Shakespearean. We know that *Henry VIII* was performed by the King's Men in the same year that they acted *Cardenno* and probably *The Two Noble Kinsmen,* for it was the play they were putting on at the Globe when that theater burned down on 29 June 1613. *Henry VIII,* therefore, belongs to the same year as Shakespeare's other probable collaborations with his successor, John Fletcher. The only contemporary evidence for the authorship of this play, as for several others, is its inclusion by Heminges and Condell in the First Folio. Shakespeare's authorship was not questioned, however, until the middle of the nineteenth century, when two English scholars, James Spedding and Samuel Hickson, working independently, analyzed the verse of the play and found only about one-third of it characteristic of Shakespeare and the other two-thirds much more like the verse of John Fletcher. Since then most students of Shakespeare have agreed that the play probably was a collaboration between the two dramatists of the King's company. But the question is not settled; in recent years there have been several studies asserting Shakespeare's sole authorship.

Timon of Athens is one of Shakespeare's poorer plays. Except for its appearance in the Folio, its early history is a blank. There are no records of its early performance in the form in which it appears in the Folio; the first known dramatic production is that of the text prepared in 1678 by Thomas Shadwell, who rewrote and expanded it, and most of the later productions are of some altered version. The Folio text of the play shows confusion in a great number of the lines, and the structure is incoherent—many scenes and passages that the development of the action leads one to expect are omitted. These characteristics have led most scholars to conclude that Shakespeare left the play unfinished, and there is some bibliographical evidence that Heminges and Condell did not originally intend to include it in the Folio. It has often been contended that the Folio text of *Timon* includes the work of some other playwright who was hired to complete the play from Shakespeare's rough draft, but there has never been any agreement on the identity of such a reviser or even agreement that there was one.

The Folio of 1623, the standard, if not unquestionable, canon of Shakespeare's dramatic work, was reprinted three times in the seventeenth century—in 1632, 1663–64, and 1685. The Second, Third, and Fourth Folios are basically reprints of the First, but in the second issue of the Third Folio in 1664 and again in the Fourth Folio in 1685 seven new plays are added. On the title page the new departure was announced:

> And unto this Impression is added seven Playes, never before Printed in Folio. *viz.*
> > *Pericles* Prince of *Tyre.*
> > The *London Prodigall.*
> > The History of *Thomas* Lᵈ. *Cromwell.*
> > Sir *John Oldcastle* Lord *Cobham.*
> > The *Puritan Widow.*
> > A *York-shire* Tragedy.
> > The Tragedy of *Locrine.*

All of these plays had been previously printed in quartos, some attributed to William Shakespeare on the title page and others only to W.S. Of the seven, only *Pericles* is now generally thought to be properly at-

tributed, at least in part. The others were publishers'
frauds, or mistakes, or in some cases perhaps confusions
with another dramatist whose initials were W.S.—
Wentworth Smith, or a hazy William Smith, or the
actor William Sly.

A few other plays were printed at some time in the
seventeenth century as Shakespeare's or attributed to
him in the Stationers' Register or in a publisher's list.
The chief ones are:

> *The Merry Devil of Edmonton*
> *The Birth of Merlin*
> *Edward III*

These three plays, plus those added to the Third Folio (*Pericles* excepted), form a group of nine generally
called the Shakespeare apocrypha. Various of them
have been included in editions of the works of Shakespeare in the eighteenth century and sometimes in the
nineteenth. But in good modern editions the only
plays outside the First Folio to be printed as canonical
are *Pericles, The Two Noble Kinsmen,* and the single
scene from *Sir Thomas More.*

CHAPTER 8

Shakespeare's Reputation

THE reputation of Shakespeare as the greatest writer
in the English language is so firmly established now
that one seldom hears it questioned. In most civilized
countries examples of his work, in translation or in the
original, are a part of the school curriculum; millions
of copies of his plays are sold in hundreds of different
editions and translations; productions of the tragedies
and comedies, and less often of the histories, are staged
every year in professional and amateur theaters in
almost every part of the world.

Knowledge of such evidence of Shakespeare's world-
wide reputation has been a commonplace for so many
years now that readers and often writers have tended
to exaggerate the appreciation of his accomplishment
in his own day. Occasional tributes of the late sixteenth
and early seventeenth centuries are taken to be more
representative than they really were because they conform to our modern evaluation and therefore seem inevitable. One of the most respected among twentieth-
century critics and scholars fell into this trap when he
asserted:

In his own day, Shakspere was one of the best-known figures in England. He was held in high esteem, both as a man and as a poet, while in his capacity of dramatic author he was not only immensely popular, but was rated at something like his true value by most persons of taste and judgment.

Betrayed by the same compelling urge to find modern values three and one-half centuries ago, the author of the most compendious history of Shakespeare criticism said:

The general average estimate of the century [i.e. 1598–1694], however, was that Shakespeare was England's greatest, because most universal, poet—perhaps the world's greatest poet, because in drama he rivalled, if not surpassed, the Greek tragedians and the Latin comedians, and his stream of narrative verse flowed as smoothly as Ovid's.

Both these writers have been misled, like so many others, by the difficulty of projecting themselves imaginatively into another time with alien values and standards. Overwhelmed by the unmistakable genius of William Shakespeare, they have taken occasional tributes to him by his contemporaries as illustrations of a general estimate. It is necessary to know that these two quotations, and many others like them, are in fact based on the three most famous examples of high praise of Shakespeare in the sixteenth and seventeenth centuries: that published by Francis Meres in 1598, by Ben Jonson in 1623, and by John Dryden in 1668 and later. The general conviction that these panegyrics are just has deluded modern writers into asserting that they were also typical.

The statement about "the average general estimate" in the second quotation is obviously derived from the comments of Francis Meres, and since many other such statements have the same source, it is illuminating to note what Meres really said. His remarks when quoted are always heavily cut, and—even more unfortunately —they are never presented in the context in which they appeared. The facts are these. In 1598 Francis Meres, an obscure English clergyman, published a book called *Palladis Tamia. Wits Treasury,* a fat little volume of over 600 pages into which he gathered hundreds of commonplaces—similes, allusions, anecdotes, quotations—all classified into subject sections: God's Providence, The Justice of God, Preachers, Sermons, Parents, Women, Virtue, Gluttony, Riches, Braggarts, Memory, and more than a hundred other categories. *Palladis Tamia* is really a commonplace book of the sort kept by a high proportion of the readers and students of the time, into which they copied all sorts of material they thought they might want to remember. A surprising number have survived. Many of them eventually got published, and there are hundreds of unpublished manuscript commonplace books extant in the great libraries with large Renaissance holdings.

The only feature of Meres' collection that is unusual or even very interesting is a sixteen-page section called "A comparatiue discourse of our English Poets, with the *Greeke, Latine, and Italian Poets,*" a section probably compiled in imitation of a book composed by Richard Carew two or three years before called *The Excellency of the English Tongue.* In this part of *Palladis Tamia* Francis Meres sets off a large number of English writers against Greek, Roman, and Italian writers, regularly implying that the Englishmen are as good as the foreigners. Often his comparisons exhibit more patriotism than critical discrimination, and his

consistent purpose is quite evidently to find Englishmen to pair with famous classic and Italian writers. A
few quotations from this section of his compendium
will show Francis Meres' purpose and illustrate his
judgment.

As Greece had three Poets of great antiquity,
Orpheus, Linus and *Musæus;* and *Italy,* other
three auncient Poets, *Liuius Andronicus, Ennius
& Plautus:* so hath England three auncient Poets,
Chaucer, Gower and *Lydgate.*

As *Homer* is reputed the Prince of Greek Poets;
and *Petrarch* of Italian Poets: so *Chaucer* is accounted the God of English Poets.

. . .

Ouid writ a Chronicle from the beginning of
the world to his own time, that is, to the raign of
Augustus the Emperour: so hath *Harding* the
Chronicler (after his maner of old harsh riming)
from *Adam* to his time, that is, to the raigne of
King Edward the fourth.

. . .

As the Greeke tongue is made famous and eloquent by *Homer, Hesiod, Euripedes, Aeschilus,
Sophocles, Pindarus, Phocylides* and *Aristophanes;*
and the Latine tongue by *Virgill, Ouid, Horace,
Silius Italicus, Lucanus, Lucretius, Ausonius* and
Claudianus: so the English tongue is mightily en-
riched, and gorgeouslie inuested in rare ornaments and resplendent abiliments by sir *Philip
Sidney, Spencer, Daniel, Drayton, Warner, Shakespeare, Marlow* and *Chapman.*

. . .

As *Sophocles* was called a Bee for the sweetnes
of his tongue: so in *Charles Fitz-Ieffries Drake,
Drayton* is termed *Golden-mouth'd,* for the purity
and pretiousnesse of his stile and phrase.

As *Accius, M. Attilius* and *Milithus* were called *Tragœdiographi,* because they writ Tragedies: so may wee truly terme *Michael Drayton Tragœdiographus,* for his passionate penning the downfals of valiant *Robert of Normandy,* chast *Matilda,* and great *Gaueston.*

. . .

As *Euripedes* is the most sententious among the Greek Poets: so is *Warner* amōg our English Poets.

As the soule of *Euphorbus* was thought to liue in *Pythagoras:* so the sweete wittie soule of *Ouid* liues in mellifluous & hony-tongued *Shakespeare,* witnes his *Venus* and *Adonis,* his *Lucrece,* his sugred Sonnets among his priuate friends, &c.

As *Plautus* and *Seneca* are accounted the best for Comedy and Tragedy among the Latines: so *Shakespeare* among yᵉ English is the most excellent in both kinds for the stage; for Comedy witnes his *Gētlemē of Verona,* his *Errors,* his *Loue labors lost,* his *Loue labours wonne,* his *Midsummers night dreame,* & his *Merchant of Venice:* for Tragedy his *Richard the 2. Richard the 3. Henry the 4. King Iohn, Titus Andronicus* and his *Romeo and Iuliet.*

As *Epius Stolo* said, that the Muses would speake with *Plautus* tongue, if they would speak Latin: so I say that the Muses would speak with *Shakespeares* fine filed phrase, if they would speake English.

. . .

As Italy had *Dante, Boccace, Petrarch, Tasso, Celiano* and *Ariosto:* so England had *Mathew Roydon, Thomas Atchelow, Thomas Watson, Thomas Kid, Robert Greene* & *George Peele.*

. . .

As these Tragicke Poets flourished in Greece, *Aeschylus, Euripedes, Sophocles, Alexander Aetolus, Achæus Erithriæus, Astydamus Atheniēsis, Apollodorus Tarsensis, Nicomachus Phrygius, Thespis Atticus,* and *Timon Apolloniates;* and these among the Latines, *Accius, M. Attilius, Pomponius Secundus* and *Seneca:* so these are our best for Tragedie, the Lorde *Buckhurst,* Doctor *Leg* of Cambridge, Doctor *Edes* of Oxforde, maister *Edward Ferris,* the Authour of the *Mirrour for Magistrates, Marlow, Peele, Watson, Kid, Shakespeare, Drayton, Chapman, Decker,* and *Beniamin Iohnson.*

. . .

The best Poets for Comedy among the Greeks are these, *Menander, Aristophanes, Eupolis Atheniensis, Alexis Terius, Nicostratus, Amipsias Atheniensis, Anaxādrides Rhodius, Aristonymus, Archippus Atheniesis* and *Callias Atheniensis;* and among the Latines, *Plautus, Terence, Næuius, Sext. Turpilius, Licinius Imbrex,* and *Virgilius Romanus:* so the best for Comedy amongst vs bee, *Edward* Earle of Oxforde, Doctor *Gager* of Oxforde, Maister *Rowley* once a rare Scholler of learned Pembrooke Hall in Cambridge, Maister *Edwardes* one of her Maiesties Chappell, eloquent and wittie *Iohn Lilly, Lodge, Gascoyne, Greene, Shakespeare, Thomas Nash, Thomas Heywood, Anthony Mundye* our best plotter, *Chapman, Porter, Wilson, Hathway,* and *Henry Chettle.*

The scattered extracts quoted constitute a total of less than three out of the sixteen pages of Meres' section matching English writers with Greek, Roman, and Italian ones; he thought up more than forty other ways to compare them, but in all the comparisons the method and purpose are the same. *Palladis Tamia* shows that Francis Meres knew a good deal about the work of Shakespeare and that he was enthusiastic about it, but the short extracts generally quoted from his book obscure the fact that he was also informed and enthusiastic about the work of Drayton, Spenser, Sidney, Daniel, and other Englishmen. Indeed Meres mentioned Michael Drayton more often than he did Shakespeare, and wrote more lines about his work. In his list of "the best for Comedy amongst vs" he names sixteen dramatists besides Shakespeare, and in his list of the best for tragedy, twelve, and at least half the dramatists so praised seem very obscure to us now.

To make an honest estimate of Shakespeare's reputation in his own time one must also note that though Meres is resounding in his praise, no other example of such unqualified enthusiasm is known during the dramatist's lifetime, and none appeared at the time of his death. The documents set out in the preceding chapters do show that Shakespeare must have been fairly well known in his time, and the editions of his plays and the tributes of Heminges and Condell show that he was not unappreciated. It is a gross exaggeration, however, to say that in his own day he "was rated at something like his true value by most persons of taste and judgment." In that day no writer for the contemporary theaters could achieve such a towering reputation as Shakespeare has now, and a careful examination of the recorded opinions of his contemporaries shows that though the writers of the early seventeenth century did refer to Shakespeare and sometimes praise his work, they wrote more of Ben Jonson, and they praised him more.

It is interesting, for a variety of reasons, to note that the great praiser of Shakespeare in the decade after his death was this same rival playwright, Ben Jonson. Jonson's own plays were composed on principles almost diametrically opposed to Shakespeare's; he wrote primarily for the private theater audience, not for the public theaters as Shakespeare usually had done; he was highly successful with the court audience for which he composed the most and the best of the court masques; and he was famous as a learned writer to whom both Oxford and Cambridge gave honorary degrees. In spite of the fact that Jonson's principles and interests were so different from Shakespeare's and the fact that he more than once criticized Shakespeare's methods, Jonson wrote for the First Folio verses that are fervent in their praise.

> To draw no enuy *(Shakespeare)* on thy name,
>   Am I thus ample to thy Booke, and Fame:
> While I confesse thy writings to be such,
>   As neither *Man,* nor *Muse,* can praise too much.
>   .   .   .
>   . . . Soule of the Age!
>   The applause! delight! the wonder of our Stage!
> My *Shakespeare,* rise; . . .
>   .   .   .
> For, if I thought my iudgement were of yeeres,
>   I should commit thee surely with thy peeres,
> And tell, how farre thou didst our *Lily* out-shine,
>   Or sporting *Kid,* or *Marlowes* mighty line.
> And though thou hadst small *Latine,* and lesse
>   *Greeke,*
>   From thence to honour thee, I would not seeke
> For names; but call forth thund'ring *Æschilus,*
>   *Euripides,* and *Sophocles* to vs,
> *Paccuuius, Accius,* him of *Cordoua* dead,
>   To life againe, to heare thy Buskin tread,
> And shake a Stage: Or, when thy Sockes were on,
>   Leaue thee alone, for the comparison
> Of all, that insolent *Greece,* or haughtie *Rome*
>   sent forth, or since did from their ashes come.

Triumph, my *Britaine,* thou hast one to showe,
    To whom all Scenes of *Europe* homage owe.
    He was not of an age, but for all time!

This ringing praise, higher and more discriminating
than that of Francis Meres, does indeed accord with
the common estimate of later times, but in the first
quarter of the seventeenth century it is unique. In the
extant writings of these years Jonson himself is more
widely and more resoundingly praised than is Shakespeare; to the great majority of the men of education
and taste who wrote the books of the time, Jonson's
satiric comedies, his learned tragedies, and his splendid
court masques usually seemed greater achievements
than Shakespeare's plays. Of the classically educated
writers of the early seventeenth century, not many besides Jonson could perceive that in spite of his "small
Latine, and lesse Greeke" Shakespeare was unsurpassed
among them.

In the decade before the closing of the theaters at
the beginning of the Civil War, critical opinion as expressed by English writers began more and more to
assert that the English theater had produced three
great contributors to the drama; they are commonly
grouped together, and often they are called "the great
triumvirate" or "the happy triumvirate." The three
are Jonson, Shakespeare, and Beaumont and Fletcher
—the last two commonly treated as one writer. When
one of these men is exalted above the others, it is most
often Jonson, but by no means always.

The same general taste is reflected in the nearly 200
extant records of the performances of particular plays
in the London theaters and at court during 1616–42,
except that they show more performances for the plays
of Beaumont and Fletcher than for those of either
Jonson or Shakespeare—more than twice as many.

Since most of these performance records come from the court and the Blackfriars Theatre, it is possible that a greater preference for Shakespeare's plays may have been evidenced at the Globe, but scarcely half a dozen records of the performance of particular plays at the Globe in this period have survived, and one can only guess that the public-theater audience may have shown more preference for Shakespeare's plays.

In the first decade after the reopening of the London theaters in 1660, the preference for Beaumont and Fletcher still obtained. In 1668 the principal playwright of the time said of Beaumont and Fletcher:

> Their Playes are now the most pleasant and frequent entertainments of the Stage; two of theirs being acted through the year for one of *Shakespheare's* or *Johnsons:* the reason is, because there is a certain gayety in their Comedies, and Pathos in their more serious Playes, which suits generally with all mens humours. *Shakespeares* language is likewise a little obsolete, and *Ben Johnson's* wit comes short of theirs.

In the last half of the seventeenth century the author of the above passage was the man most responsible for the formation of general critical opinion about the drama. John Dryden, an active man of the theater, deeply interested in the critical problems of the drama, was made poet laureate in 1670. He had a vast admiration for Ben Jonson, whom he called "the greatest man of the last age" and "the most learned and judicious Writer which any theater ever had." But in spite of his studied critical judgment, Dryden was even more attracted to the work of Shakespeare than of Jonson; as he put it in his famous critical essay *Of Dramatick Poesie,* first published in 1668:

If I would compare him [Jonson] with *Shakespeare,* I must acknowledge him the more correct poet, but *Shakespeare* the greater wit. *Shakespeare* was the *Homer,* or Father of our Dramatic Poets; *Johnson* was the *Virgil,* the pattern of elaborate writing; I admire him, but I love Shakespeare.

Dryden's influence was great, and in the last two decades of the seventeenth century the general estimate of Shakespeare's accomplishment was rising; though Jonson was still mentioned more often, the difference between them was less than before.

During the last third of the seventeenth century there developed a phenomenon in the treatment of Shakespeare's plays that lasted for about two hundred years. This phenomenon was a sharp distinction between the plays as performed in the theaters and as printed for readers. The editions of the complete plays that were successively issued for readers—in 1663–64, 1685, 1709, 1725, 1733, 1744, 1747, 1753, 1765, and so on—were reprints of the text of the Folio of 1623 with minor adjustments and revisions. But the plays performed in the theaters were commonly heavily cut and frequently completely rewritten versions of Shakespeare's plays, often with several characters dropped and new ones inserted. William Davenant revised *Measure for Measure, Macbeth,* and *Hamlet;* Dryden revised *The Tempest;* Nahum Tate rewrote *King Lear, Richard II,* and *Coriolanus;* John Lacy rewrote *The Taming of the Shrew;* Shadwell redid *Timon of Athens* and Edward Ravenscroft *Titus Andronicus;* John Crowne rewrote 2 and 3 *Henry VI; A Midsummer Night's Dream* was rewritten into an opera called *The Fairy Queen.*

All these rewritings of Shakespeare's plays for the contemporary stage were prepared before 1700, but

207

the process continued during the eighteenth and nine-teenth centuries. Never was a play acted just as Shake-speare had written it, and often the adapter cut more than a third of the play, or combined two of Shake-speare's plays with new material to make a new piece, as Davenant did when he made *The Law against Lovers* out of parts of *Measure for Measure* and *Much Ado*.

But however mutilated and vulgarized were the ver-sions of Shakespeare's plays performed during the Res-toration and the eighteenth century, and however in-adequate the many editions offered to the readers in this time, they encouraged and exploited the recogni-tion of Shakespeare as England's greatest dramatist. In the first half of the eighteenth century his plays were constantly performed in the major London theaters, sometimes constituting one-fifth of all performances in a given year. Complete editions of the plays were issued twelve times, and cheap editions of single plays were poured out, in one two-year period amounting to more than 100 different printings of separate plays. This widespread exploitation of Shakespeare's plays was in part the result of restrictions on productions of new comedies and tragedies made by the Licensing Act of 1737 and of a peculiar situation in the London pub-lishing world, but increased interest in Shakespeare was nonetheless fostered by it.

This burgeoning interest was most conspicuously sustained and promoted by David Garrick, the greatest actor of his time, who became famous in a number of Shakespearean roles, who was painted by the most emi-nent contemporary artists posed beside a statue of Shakespeare or performing a role in one of his plays, and who was the leading figure in the great Shakespeare Jubilee at Stratford in September 1769. The four-day celebration brought hosts of distinguished or notorious visitors to Stratford and was described, praised, or ridiculed in multitudes of pamphlets and newspaper stories. The elaborate costume pageant that was rained out in a near-flood at Stratford was later staged at Drury Lane Theatre in London and ran for ninety performances. Much of this Jubilee activity was absurd, and advertising for Garrick and profit for Stratford are obvious among its motives, but for all its contriving, it symbolizes the advent of the unrestrained admiration for Shakespeare, often unthinking and gullible, and properly called Bardolatry.

Bardolatry elicited not only constant audiences for performances in the theaters and buyers for editions of the plays, but fake relics, invented portraits, forged papers, and even manufactured plays and poems and literary fragments. Objects made from pieces of the mulberry tree in the garden at New Place were issued in numbers great enough to consume a score of mulberry trees; old portraits were touched up to look a little like the engraving in the Folio and palmed off as likenesses of The Bard; books from his alleged library carrying the notes of the Master turned up. Most sensational were the manuscripts produced by William Ireland in the 1790's and publicized by his innocent but gullible father, Samuel Ireland the antiquary. William quietly manufactured for Shakespeare deeds, letters, a declaration of faith, a love poem to Anne Hathaway with a lock of the poet's hair, an early manuscript of *King Lear,* a fragment of *Hamlet,* and an unknown play called *Vortigern and Rowena.* For a time most people were taken in and there was a great furor over the magnificent discoveries; James Boswell, for example, came to kneel before the forgeries and kiss them. But young Ireland was not a very good forger, and when he was eventually exposed, he confessed.

The affair of the Ireland forgeries is a good illustration of the consequences of Shakespeare idolatry, of the excesses to which it is likely to lead. Along with a just appreciation of Shakespeare's accomplishment, there grew up in the late eighteenth and the nineteenth centuries an unreasoning adulation and a tendency to approach Shakespeare's works as if they were the creations of a god rather than a man. Many persons wanted relics, and they assumed that every play and poem from his hand must be perfection. Consequently any line or scene or play which did not meet the reader's idea of perfection was likely to be rejected as spurious —the work of collaborators, or insertions by the actors, or blunders by the printers. Prudish readers rejected the brothel scenes in *Pericles* and the bawdy allusions in the comedies; solemn readers rejected the comic scenes in the tragedies; snobbish readers rejected vulgar scenes; and squeamish readers rejected the mutilations in *King Lear* and *Titus Andronicus*. There were disadvantages to the glorification of Shakespeare which had become widespread by the beginning of the nineteenth century; indeed, the tendency to assume that the superhuman Shakespeare can have written only what meets a particular writer's approval has by no means disappeared from modern criticism.

Throughout the nineteenth century the plays of Shakespeare continued to be a mainstay of the theaters and an unfailing source of interest and often of profit to publishers and critics. In the theaters most of the greatest actors made Shakespearean roles vehicles for their fame. Unfortunately, in London, which set the styles, during most of the century the theaters were too large and the stages so overloaded with scenery and properties that cut versions of the plays were still a necessity. Not only was a flowing action impossible when scene changes were both elaborate and numerous, but the livestock in *A Midsummer Night's Dream* and *As You Like It* or the cathedral in *Much Ado* or the palace in *Henry VIII* in many productions of Macready and Kean, of Henry Irving and Beerbohm Tree, divided the audience interest with the star, and most of the subtleties of the plays were lost.

Toward the end of the century, however, protests against the overproduction and the cutting of the plays began to swell. Perhaps the most influential protester was William Poel, an actor who founded the Elizabethan Stage Society and put on a number of semiprofessional performances of uncut Shakespearean and other Elizabethan plays without scenery. Poel's productions, staged at intervals during the last decade or so of the nineteenth century and the first quarter of the twentieth, were never popular and they generally lost money, but gradually he persuaded producers like Granville-Barker and a few others that his basic ideas were sound, and the spectacle productions ceased to monopolize the theater.

Poel's conception that Shakespeare's plays were most effective when produced more or less as the author planned them to be is certainly not universally followed even now, but most productions have moved in that direction, and a few, mostly at the Shakespeare festival theaters, go almost far enough to have pleased Poel. Annual seasons of Shakespeare productions like those at Stratford-upon-Avon, Stratford in Ontario, Stratford in Connecticut, and Ashland, Oregon, at least involve producers and advisers who know something of the kind of production Shakespeare planned, though the compromises they feel they must make to avoid the prejudices of modern audiences or modern backers or to accommodate their stars often disappoint the purists. In the regular London and New York theaters, Shakespeare productions do not provide such a high proportion of the annual offerings as they did in nineteenth-century London, but the total number of performances in all theaters in any given year is far higher now than it has ever been before.

New printings of Shakespeare's plays are also more frequently issued and more widely distributed than ever before. Not only are there now more scholarly editions prepared for the careful student, but popular editions for general readers and for the schools are sold in vast quantities, especially since the advent in America of the paperbacks.

All this widespread reliance on the appeal of the plays of Shakespeare in the theater and in the study is eloquent testimony to the extent of his reputation in our time. No informed student would contend that Bardolatry is extinct, but genuine understanding of the plays of the First Folio has been attained by millions.

During and immediately after Shakespeare's lifetime the learned Ben Jonson may well have seemed to most articulate commentators to be the greatest English dramatist. But Jonson himself knew better; and his own estimate expressed in his verses for the First Folio has proved to be the most prophetic statement about Shakespeare:

He was not of an age, but for all time!

Bibliography

General

Bentley, Gerald Eades, *The Jacobean and Caroline Stage*, 5 vols. Oxford, the Clarendon Press, 1941–56.

Chambers, E. K., *The Elizabethan Stage*, 4 vols. Oxford, the Clarendon Press, 1923.

——*William Shakespeare: A Study of Facts and Problems*, 2 vols. Oxford, the Clarendon Press, 1930.

——*Shakespearean Gleanings*, Oxford, Oxford University Press, 1944.

Halliday, F. E., *A Shakespeare Companion 1550–1950*, London, Duckworth, 1952.

——*Shakespeare, a Pictorial Biography*, London, Thames and Hudson, 1956.

Lewis, B. Roland, *The Shakespeare Documents: Facsimiles, Transliterations, Translations & Commentary*, 2 vols. Stanford, Stanford University Press, 1940–41.

Onions, C. T., ed., *Shakespeare's England: An Account of the Life & Manners of His Age*, 2 vols. Oxford, the Clarendon Press, 1916–17.

Wilson, F. P., *The Plague in Shakespeare's London*, Oxford, the Clarendon Press, 1927.

Wright, Louis B., *Middle-Class Culture in Elizbethan England*, Chapel Hill, University of North Carolina Press, 1935.

CHAPTER 1. Shakespearean Biography

Bacon, Delia, *The Philosophy of the Plays of Shakspere Unfolded*, London, Groombridge and Sons, 1857.

Churchill, R. C., *Shakespeare and His Betters: A History and a Criticism of the Attempts Which Have Been Made to Prove That Shakespeare's Works Were Written by Others*, Bloomington, Indiana, Indiana University Press, 1959.

Donnelly, Ignatius, *The Great Cryptogram*, New York, R. S. Peal, 1888.

Friedman, William and Elizabeth, *The Shakespeare Ciphers Examined*, Cambridge, Cambridge University Press, 1957.

Harbage, Alfred, "Sweet Will and Gentle Marlowe," *New York Times Book Review*, 12 June 1955.

Looney, J. Thomas, *"Shakespeare" Identified in Edward de Vere the Seventeenth Earl of Oxford*, London, Frederick A. Stokes, 1920.

Robertson, J. M., *The Baconian Heresy*, New York, E. P. Dutton, 1913.

Ross, William, *The Story of Anne Whateley and William Shaxpere*, Glasgow, W. & R. Holmes, 1939.

Sola Pinto, Vivian de, ed., *English Biography in the Seventeenth Century: Selected Short Lives*, London, Harrap, 1951.

Stauffer, Donald A., *English Biography before 1700*, Cambridge, Massachusetts, Harvard University Press, 1930.

Wadsworth, Frank W., *The Poacher from Stratford: A Partial Account of the Controversy over the Authorship of Shakespeare's Plays*, Berkeley and Los Angeles, University of California Press, 1958.

CHAPTER 2. Shakespeare in Stratford-upon-Avon

Baldwin, Thomas Whitfield, *William Shakspere's Small Latine & Lesse Greeke*, 2 vols. Urbana, Illinois, University of Illinois Press, 1944.

Fripp, Edgar I., *Minutes and Accounts of the Corporation of Stratford-upon-Avon,* 4 vols. Oxford, Dugdale Society, 1921–29.

——*Shakespeare's Haunts near Stratford,* London, Oxford University Press, 1929.

——*Shakespeare, Man and Artist,* 2 vols. London, Oxford University Press, 1938.

——*Shakespeare's Stratford,* London, Oxford University Press, 1928.

Hotson, Leslie, *I, William Shakespeare Do Appoint Thomas Russell, Esquire* . . . London, Jonathan Cape, 1937.

——*Shakespeare's Sonnets Dated and Other Essays,* London, Rupert Hart-Davis, 1949.

Styles, Philip, *The Borough of Stratford-upon-Avon and the Parish of Alveston,* London, Oxford University Press, 1946.

CHAPTER 3. In London

Hotson, Leslie, *Shakespeare's Sonnets Dated and Other Essays,* London, Rupert Hart-Davis, 1949.

——*Shakespeare versus Shallow,* Boston, Little, Brown, and Company, 1931.

Wallace, Charles W., "Shakespeare and His London Associates, as Revealed in Recently Discovered Documents," *University of Nebraska Studies, 10* (1910), 261–360.

CHAPTER 4. The Actor

Baker, Oliver, *In Shakespeare's Warwickshire and the Unknown Years,* London, Simpkin Marshall, 1937.

Baldwin, Thomas Whitfield, *The Organization and Personnel of the Shakespearean Company,* Princeton, Princeton University Press, 1927.

Chambers, E. K., *The Elizabethan Stage,* 4 vols. Oxford, the Clarendon Press, 1923.

Leishman, J. B., ed., *The Three Parnassus Plays (1598–1601),* London, Ivor Nicholson & Watson, 1949.

Stevenson, Robert, *Shakespeare's Religious Frontier,* The Hague, Martinus Nijhoff, 1958.

Wilson, F. P., *The Plague in Shakespeare's London,* Oxford, the Clarendon Press, 1927.

CHAPTER 5. The Playwright

Baldwin, Thomas Whitfield, *The Organization and Personnel of the Shakespearean Company,* Princeton, Princeton University Press, 1927.

Bentley, G. E., "Shakespeare and the Blackfriars Theatre," *Shakespeare Survey, 1* (1948), 38–50.

Chambers, E. K., *The Elizabethan Stage,* 4 vols. Oxford, the Clarendon Press, 1923.

Doran, Madeleine, *Endeavors of Art: A Study of Form in Elizabethan Drama,* Madison, University of Wisconsin Press, 1954.

Granville-Barker, Harley, *Prefaces to Shakespeare* [*Hamlet, Lear, Merchant of Venice, Antony and Cleopatra, Cymbeline, Othello, Coriolanus, Julius Caesar, Romeo and Juliet, Love's Labour's Lost*], 2 vols. Princeton, Princeton University Press, 1946–47.

Greg, W. W., *Dramatic Documents from the Elizabethan Playhouses,* 2 vols. Oxford, the Clarendon Press, 1931.

——— ed., *Henslowe's Diary,* 2 vols. London, A. H. Bullen, 1904–08.

Harbage, Alfred, *Shakespeare's Audience,* New York, Columbia University Press, 1941.

Hodges, C. Walter, *The Globe Restored: A Study of the Elizabethan Theatre,* London, Ernest Benn, 1953.

Hotson, Leslie, *Shakespeare's Motley,* London, Rupert Hart-Davis, 1952.

Nagler, A. M., *Shakespeare's Stage,* New Haven, Yale University Press, 1958.

Sisson, Charles J., ed., *Believe as You List by Philip Massinger. 1631,* Malone Society Reprints, Oxford, Oxford University Press, 1927.

CHAPTER 6. The Nondramatic Poet

Brooke, Tucker, *Shakespeare's Sonnets,* London, Oxford University Press, 1936.
Hubler, Edward, *The Sense of Shakespeare's Sonnets,* Princeton, Princeton University Press, 1952.
Rollins, Hyder Edward, *The Poems. New Variorum Edition,* Philadelphia, Lippincott, 1938.
————*The Sonnets. New Variorum Edition,* 2 vols. Philadelphia, Lippincott, 1944.
Stopes, Charlotte Carmichael, *The Life of Henry, Third Earl of Southampton, Shakespeare's Patron,* Cambridge, Cambridge University Press, 1922.

CHAPTER 7. Shakespeare and the Printers

Arber, Edward, ed., *A Transcript of the Registers of the Company of Stationers of London; 1554–1640 A.D.,* 5 vols. London, privately printed, 1875–94.
Brooke, C. F. Tucker, ed., *The Shakespeare Apocrypha. Being a Collection of Fourteen Plays Which Have Been Ascribed to Shakespeare,* Oxford, the Clarendon Press, 1908.
Chambers, E. K., *The Elizabethan Stage,* 4 vols. Oxford, the Clarendon Press, 1923.
Greg, W. W., *A Bibliography of the English Printed Drama to the Restoration,* 4 vols. London, the Bibliographical Society, 1939–59.
————*The Shakespeare First Folio: Its Bibliographical and Textual History,* Oxford, the Clarendon Press, 1955.
————*Some Aspects and Problems of London Publishing between 1550 and 1650,* Oxford, the Clarendon Press, 1956.
Kirschbaum, Leo, "The Copyright of Elizabethan Plays," *Library,* 5th ser. *14* (1959), 231–50.
Kökeritz, Helge, ed., *Mr. William Shakespeares Comedies, Histories, & Tragedies. A Facsimile Edition Prepared by*

Helge Kökeritz with an Introduction by Charles Tyler
Prouty, New Haven, Yale University Press, 1954.

Maxwell, Baldwin, *Studies in the Shakespeare Apocrypha,*
New York, King's Crown Press, 1956.

Ransom, Harry, *The First Copyright Statute: An Essay on
an Act for the Encouragement of Learning, 1710,* Austin,
University of Texas Press, 1956.

CHAPTER 8. Shakespeare's Reputation

Allen, Don Cameron, ed., *Palladis Tamia (1598) by Francis
Meres,* New York, Scholars Facsimiles & Reprints, 1938.

Babcock, R. W., *The Genesis of Shakespeare Idolatry, 1766–
1799,* Chapel Hill, University of North Carolina Press,
1931.

Bentley, Gerald Eades, *Shakespeare & Jonson: Their Repu-
tations in the Seventeenth Century Compared,* 2 vols. Chicago, University of Chicago Press, 1945.

Brown, Ivor, and George Fearon, *Amazing Monument: A
Short History of the Shakespeare Industry,* London, Heine-
mann, 1939.

Halliday, F. E., *The Cult of Shakespeare,* London, Duckworth, 1957.

Munro, John, ed., *The Shakspere Allusion Book: A Collection of Allusions to Shakspere from 1591 to 1700,* 2 vols.
London, Oxford University Press, 1932.

Ralli, Augustus, *A History of Shakespearian Criticism,* 2 vols.
London, Oxford University Press, 1932.

Scouten, Arthur H., "The Increase in Popularity of Shakespeare's Plays in the Eighteenth Century: A *Caveat* for
Interpretors of Stage History," *Shakespeare Quarterly,* 7
(1956), 188–202.

Speaight, Robert, *William Poel and the Elizabethan Revival,*
Cambridge, Massachusetts, Harvard University Press, 1954.

Spencer, Hazelton, *Shakespeare Improved: The Restoration
Versions in Quarto and on the Stage,* Cambridge, Massachusetts, Harvard University Press, 1927.

Quoted Documents and Books

Page

7a   Aubrey MS 8, Bodleian Library, Oxford. Facsimile printed in B. Roland Lewis, *The Shakespeare Documents* (Stanford, 1940–41), *1*, 318.

7b   Manuscript in University Library, Edinburgh. Transcription in J. O. Halliwell-Phillipps, *Outlines of the Life of Shakespeare* (London, 1890), *2*, 286.

8   [Richard Ryan], *Dramatic Table Talk* (London, 1825), *2*, 156–57.

10a   Charles Gildon, *The Lives and Characters of the English Dramatick Poets* (London, 1698), p. 126.

10b   John Dennis, *The Comicall Gallant* (London, 1702), Epistle.

11a   Nicholas Rowe, ed., *The Works of Mr. William Shakespear* (London, 1709), *1*, viii–ix.

11b   Charles Gildon, "Remarks on the Plays of Shakespear," in Nicholas Rowe, *The Works of Mr. William Shakespear* (London, 1710), *7*, 291.

13   Aubrey MS 6, Bodleian Library, Oxford.

Page

14a C. E. Doble, *Remarks and Collections of Thomas Hearne* (Oxford, 1886), 2, 228.

14b S. W. Singer, ed., *Anecdotes, Observations, and Characters of Books and Men. Collected from the Conversation of Mr. Pope and Other Eminent Persons of His Time* (London, 1820), pp. 23, 269.

15 George Steevens, ed., *The Plays of William Shakespeare* (London, 1778), *1*, 203.

25 Manuscript parish register, Holy Trinity Church, Stratford-upon-Avon. Facsimile in Lewis, *Shakespeare Documents, 1*, 126.

28 Nicholas Rowe, ed., *The Works of Mr. William Shakespear* (London, 1709), *1*, ii–iii.

30 Bond on vellum, Worcester Diocesan Registry, Worcester, England. Facsimile in Lewis, *Shakespeare Documents, 1*, 160.

32 Manuscript parish register, Holy Trinity Church, Stratford-upon-Avon.

33a Ibid.

33b Ibid.

34 Nicholas Rowe, ed., *The Works of Mr. William Shakespear, 1*, v–vi.

35 Aubrey MS 6, Bodleian Library, Oxford. Facsimile in Lewis, *Shakespeare Documents, 1*, 318.

36 The original is in the Public Record Office, London. A contemporary exemplification, or copy, is in the Birthplace Museum, Stratford-upon-Avon. Facsimile in Lewis, *Shakespeare Documents, 1*, 237.

37a Miscellaneous Documents, Birthplace Museum, Stratford-upon-Avon. Facsimile in Lewis, *Shakespeare Documents, 1,* 283.

37b–39 All four letters are in the Birthplace Museum, Stratford-upon-Avon. Facsimile of the second letter in Lewis, *Shakespeare Documents, 1,* 226.

40–41 Vincent Manuscripts, College of Arms, London. Facsimile in Lewis, *Shakespeare Documents, 1,* 211.

42–43a Birthplace Museum, Stratford-upon-Avon. Facsimile in Lewis, *Shakespeare Documents, 2,* 330.

43b Court Rolls, Public Record Office, London. Transcribed in C. C. Stopes, *Shakespeare's Industry* (London, 1916), p. 269.

44 Birthplace Museum, Stratford-upon-Avon. Facsimile in Lewis, *Shakespeare Documents, 2,* 374.

45–46a Birthplace Museum, Stratford-upon-Avon. Full transcription in J. O. Halliwell-Phillipps, *Outlines of the Life of Shakespeare* (London, 1890), 2, 25–31.

46b Manuscript parish register, Holy Trinity Church, Stratford-upon-Avon.

47a Gravestone, Holy Trinity Church, Stratford-upon-Avon.

47b Ibid.

48 Public Record Office, London. Transcribed in Halliwell-Phillipps, *Outlines, 2,* 25.

49a Birthplace Museum, Stratford-upon-Avon. Facsimile in Lewis, *Shakespeare Documents, 2,* 416.

Page

49b Somerset House, London. Entire will transcribed in Halliwell-Phillipps, *A Life of William Shakespeare* (London, 1848), pp. 234–40.

50a Richard Brathwait, *Remains after Death,* appended to Patrick Hannay, *A Happy Husband,* London, 1619.

50b–51 Rowe, ed., *The Works of Mr. William Shakespear, 1,* xxxvi.

53a Birthplace Museum, Stratford-upon-Avon. Facsimile in Lewis, *Shakespeare Documents, 2,* 458.

53b–54a Birthplace Museum, Stratford-upon-Avon. Facsimile in Halliwell-Phillipps, *Outlines, 2,* 38–39.

54b–56b Birthplace Museum, Stratford-upon-Avon. Facsimiles of sample pages, Lewis, *Shakespeare Documents, 2,* 458–59, and E. K. Chambers, *William Shakespeare* (Oxford, 1930), *2,* 143.

56c Manuscript parish register, Holy Trinity Church, Stratford-upon-Avon.

57–61 Somerset House, London. Facsimilies in Lewis, *Shakespeare Documents, 2,* 482 ff., and Chambers, *William Shakespeare, 2,* 170–74.

64a Folger Shakespeare Library, Washington, D.C. Facsimile in Lewis, *Shakespeare Documents, 2,* 526.

64b Manuscript parish register, Holy Trinity Church, Stratford-upon-Avon. Facsimile in Lewis, *Shakespeare Documents, 2,* frontispiece.

66–67a Monument, Holy Trinity Church, Stratford-upon-Avon. Facsimile of rubbing in Lewis, *Shakespeare Documents, 2,* 546.

81b Manuscript parish register, St. Saviour's Southwark Church, London.

81c Manuscript fee book, St. Saviour's Southwark
Church, London.

82 Manuscript account book in the manuscripts of
the Duke of Rutland, Belvoir Castle, Leicester-
shire.

83–84 Guildhall Library, London. Facsimile in Lewis,
Shakespeare Documents, 2, 438.

85–86a Egerton MS 1787, British Museum, London. Facsimile in Lewis, *Shakespeare Documents, 2,* 446.

86b Chancery suit, Public Record Office, London. Full
transcript in C. W. Wallace, *University of Nebraska Studies, 5* (1905).

91–92 Patent Rolls, Public Record Office, London. Type
facsimile, *Malone Society Collections, 2,* Pt. III
(1909), 264–65.

94–95 Robert Greene, *Greenes Groats-worth of Wit
bought with a million of Repentance,* London,
1592.

96 Henry Chettle, *Kind-harts Dreame* (London, 1592),
"Epistle."

99–100 Declared Accounts, Public Record Office, London.
Type facsimile, *Malone Society Collections, 6*
(1961), 29.

101 *The Workes of Beniamin Jonson* (London, 1616),
sig. F6^v.

102–3 Court of Requests suit, Public Record Office, London. Printed by C. W. Wallace in *University of
Nebraska Studies, 10* (1910), 307–36.

104–5a Star Chamber Proceedings, Public Record Office, London. Printed in full by C. W. Wallace, *University of Nebraska Studies, 13* (1913), 276–83.

105b Inquisitions Post Mortem, Public Record Office, London. First printed by C. W. Wallace in *The Times* (London), 1 May 1914, p. 4.

106–7 Lord Chamberlain's Papers, Public Record Office, London. Printed in full in *Malone Society Collections, 2*, Pt. III (1931), 370–73.

108 Harleian Manuscript 5353, British Museum, London. Facsimile in Lewis, *Shakespeare Documents, 1*, 318.

109–10 Manuscript, Folger Shakespeare Library, Washington, D.C. Full transcription in J. B. Leishman, *The Three Parnassus Plays*, London, 1949.

111–12a Privy Signet Bill, Public Record Office, London. Facsimile printed in Lewis, *Shakespeare Documents, 2*, 366.

112b *The Workes of Beniamin Jonson* (London, 1616), sig. 2O3^v.

113a Lord Chamberlain's Papers, Public Record Office, London. Printed with similar documents *Malone Society Collections, 2*, Pt. III (1931), 322–26.

113b–14a Declared Accounts, Public Record Office, London. Type facsimile in *Malone Society Collections, 6* (1961), 38.

114b–15 Somerset House, London. First printed in George Chalmers, *An Apology for Believers in the Shakespeare Papers*, London, 1797.

116   Lord Chamberlain's Papers, Public Record Office, London. Printed in full in *Malone Society Collections*, 2, Pt. III (1931), 370–73.

118   *Mr. William Shakespeares Comedies, Histories, & Tragedies* (London, 1623), sig. [πB2].

124   Manuscript in Basle University Library. First printed by G. Binz, *Anglia*, 22 (1899), 456–64.

145–46   William Shakespeare, *Venus and Adonis* (London, 1593), sig. A2. Facsimile edition edited by Sir Sidney Lee, Oxford, 1905.

147a   Manuscript note by Gabriel Harvey in his copy of T. Speght, ed., *The Workes of our Antient and Lerned English Poet, G. Chaucer newly printed*, London, 1598. Now in a private collection. Facsimile in G. C. Moore Smith, *Gabriel Harvey's Marginalia*, Stratford-upon-Avon, 1913.

147b   John Weever, *Epigrammes in the Oldest Cut and Newest Fashion*, London, 1599.

148a   Manuscript Rawlinson D.398, Bodleian Library, Oxford. Reprinted in J. B. Leishman, ed., *The Three Parnassus Plays*, p. 185.

148b   Ibid. pp. 192–93.

149–50   William Shakespeare, *Lucrece* (London, 1594), sig. A2. Facsimile of this page in F. E. Halliday, *Shakespeare, a Pictorial Biography* (London, 1956), p. 54.

153a   Francis Meres, *Palladis Tamia. Wits Treasury being the second part of Wits Commonwealth* (London, 1598), Oo1^v–Oo2. Facsimile edited by Don Cameron Allen, New York, 1938.

Page

153b *Shake-speares Sonnets* (London, 1609), sig. A2. Facsimile edition ed. Sir Sidney Lee, Oxford, 1905.

163 Manuscript Registers of the Stationers' Company, Stationers Hall, London. Exact transcripts of the entries for plays are printed in W. W. Greg, *A Bibliography of the English Printed Drama to the Restoration* (London, 1939), *1*, 1–78.

167–8 Thomas Heywood, *The Rape of Lucrece* (London, 1608), sig. A2.

185 *Mr. William Shakespeares Comedies, Histories, & Tragedies* (London, 1623), sigs. A2–A2ᵛ. Facsimile edition, New Haven, 1954.

187 Ibid. sig. A3.

191 Harleian Manuscript 7368, British Museum, London. Type facsimile edition by W. W. Greg, *Malone Society Reprints*, Oxford, 1911.

193 Manuscript Registers of the Stationers' Company, Stationers Hall, London. Transcript by W. W. Greg, *A Bibliography of the English Printed Drama to the Restoration, 1*, 60–61.

195 *Mr. William Shakespear's Comedies, Histories, and Tragedies*, London, 1664. Facsimile edition, Methuen, London, 1905.

198a G. L. Kittredge, *Shakspere: An Address* (Cambridge, Massachusetts, 1916), p. 24.

198b Augustus Ralli, *A History of Shakespearian Criticism* (Oxford, 1932), *1*, 10.

200a Francis Meres, *Palladis Tamia*, sig. Nn7.

200b Ibid., sig. Nn7ᵛ.

Page

200c Ibid., sig. Nn8.

200d–1a Ibid., sig. Oo1.

201b Ibid., sigs. Oo1^v–Oo2.

201c Ibid., sig. Oo2^v.

202a Ibid., sig. Oo3.

202b Ibid., sigs. Oo3–Oo3^v.

204–5 *Mr. William Shakespeares Comedies, Histories, & Tragedies* (London, 1623), sigs. [πA4–A4^v]. Facsimile edition, New Haven, 1954.

206 John Dryden, *Of Dramatick Poesie* (London, 1668), sig. H1.

207 Ibid., sig. H1^v.

Order and Dates of the Plays

EXCEPT for those plays, now mostly lost, which were recorded in Philip Henslowe's diary, it is extremely rare for the precise date of any Elizabethan play to be known, and Shakespeare's plays share the common history: there is no contemporary record of the first production date of any of them. The dates we use are all conjectural and have been reached in a variety of ways—from occasional allusions in the plays themselves to historic events, from the dates of their appearance in print, from records of court performances, from the publication dates of sources, from mention in Meres' *Palladis Tamia*, and from a few quotations or imitations in other books and plays.

Such inferential dates cannot be very certain, and there is, not surprisingly, still disagreement among scholars about the chronology of the plays. The composition dates given here are those suggested by Sir Edmund Chambers in the most authoritative general treatment of the subject, *William Shakespeare: A Study of Facts and Problems* (Oxford, 1930), *I*, 241–532. This chronology is widely but by no means universally accepted. It should be remembered that so far as we can tell from Elizabethan comments and records, productions of the plays of professional dramatists like Shakespeare normally followed immediately upon completion of the manuscript; for a play the date of production is the date of birth.

The publication dates here listed are much more certain than the composition dates, for most editions carry the year of publication on the title pages. Occasionally, however, there is some doubt, as when the first extant edition carries a statement that it is a revised or corrected version, thus implying an earlier printing now unknown; or when the first known edition of a play is so radically different from the later ones that it is uncertain whether we have a Bad Quarto or a source play, as in the cases of *Henry VI, Part 2* and *Henry VI, Part 3*. In these instances of uncertainty, the date of first printing has been followed by a query.

First Performed		*First Printed*
1590–91	*Henry VI, Part 2*	1594?
1590–91	*Henry VI, Part 3*	1594?
1591–92	*Henry VI, Part 1*	1623
1592–93	*Richard III*	1597
1592–93	*Comedy of Errors*	1623
1593–94	*Titus Andronicus*	1594
1593–94	*Taming of the Shrew*	1623
1594–95	*Two Gentlemen of Verona*	1623
1594–95	*Love's Labour's Lost*	1598?
1594–95	*Romeo and Juliet*	1597
1595–96	*Richard II*	1597
1595–96	*A Midsummer Night's Dream*	1600
1596–97	*King John*	1623
1596–97	*The Merchant of Venice*	1600
1597–98	*Henry IV, Part 1*	1598
1597–98	*Henry IV, Part 2*	1600
1598–99	*Much Ado About Nothing*	1600
1598–99	*Henry V*	1600
1599–1600	*Julius Caesar*	1623
1599–1600	*As You Like It*	1623
1599–1600	*Twelfth Night*	1623

First Performed		First Printed
1600–01	Hamlet	1603
1600–01	The Merry Wives of Windsor	1602
1601–02	Troilus and Cressida	1609
1602–03	All's Well That Ends Well	1623
1604–05	Measure for Measure	1623
1604–05	Othello	1622
1605–06	King Lear	1608
1605–06	Macbeth	1623
1606–07	Antony and Cleopatra	1623
1607–08	Coriolanus	1623
1607–08	Timon of Athens	1623
1608–09	Pericles	1609
1609–10	Cymbeline	1623
1610–11	The Winter's Tale	1623
1611–12	The Tempest	1623
1612–13	Henry VIII	1623
1612–13	The Two Noble Kinsmen	1634

Index

granddaughter, 32, 36, 64
Bernardo, character of, 10
Betterton, Thomas, actor, 15, 28, 34
Bibliography of the English Printed Drama to the Restoration. See Greg, W. W.
Birth of Merlin, 196
Birthplace Museum. *See* Stratford-upon-Avon
Bishops, 2. *See also* London
Bishopsgate. *See* London
Bishopton, 45, 53, 59
Blackfriars District. *See* London
Blackfriars Theatre, 83, 130, 184, 186, 187, 188, 190, 192, 206; acquisition of by King's company, 115–17
Boccaccio, 201
Bodleian Library, Oxford, 219–20, 226
Bodley, Sir Thomas, 107
Bolingbroke, character of, 134
Bonaparte, Napoleon, 6
Book sellers, 96
Book stalls, 107
Boswell, James, 209
Bottom, character of, 129
Box-holders, 123
Boy actors, 8, 90, 114, 115, 116, 122, 125–28; in women's roles, 8, 90
Boy companies, 90, 115, 166, 168
Boyese, William, 72
Brabantio, character of, 139, 140
Braggart Gentleman, character of, 181
Brathwaite, Richard, *Remains after Death,* 50, 222
Brend, Nicholas, 102, 103, 105
Brend, Thomas, 105
Bridge Street. *See* Stratford-upon-Avon

British Museum, 224, 225, 227; Harleian collection, 191
Brome, Richard, 120
Bryan, George, 118
Bubonic plague. *See* Plague
Buckhurst, Thomas Sackville, Lord, 202
Bull Inn, 102
Burbage, Cuthbert, 103, 104, 106, 107, 115, 116, 125
Burbage, James, 107, 115
Burbage, Richard, 82, 89, 92, 98, 100, 101, 103, 104, 105, 106, 107, 108, 111, 112, 113, 115, 116, 118, 125, 189; as character, 109–11; death of, 186; legacy to, 59, 62
Burbage, William, 106
Burbage, Winifred, 106
Burghley, William Cecil, Lord, 151
Burton, Robert, *Anatomy of Melancholy,* 20
Bushells, Mr., 38
Butchers, 7, 18
Butler, Samuel, 13; *Hudibras,* 13
Byron, George Gordon, Lord, 18

Cade, Jack, character of, 173
Cæliano, Torquato, 156
Cage Tavern. *See* Stratford-upon-Avon
Callias Atheniensis, 202
Cambridge, town of, 162
Cambridge University, 108, 109, 110, 147, 148, 181, 202, 204; Pembroke Hall, 202; St. John's College, 108, 109, 147
Campion, Thomas, 17
Canterbury, 23; Archbishop of, 162
Capulet, Lady, character of, 128

Gertrude, character of, 19, 128, 136

Ghost, character of, 10, 136, 137

Gibson, William, *Two for the See-Saw*, 123

Gilburne, Samuel, 118; legacy to, 114

Gildon, Charles, 9–10, 11; *The Lives and Characters of the English Dramatick Poets*, 219; "Remarks on the Plays of Shakespear," 219

Globe Theatre, 43, 65, 73, 76, 80, 92, 108, 112, 115, 117, 124, 129, 130, 132, 134, 136, 140, 182, 183, 184, 186, 190, 206; building of, 102–07; burning of, 125, 194; staging at, 135–38

Gloucester, Duke of, character of, 126, 172, 181

Glove-makers, 24

Golden Age. See Heywood, Thomas

Goneril, character of, 182

Gospel Bush. *See* Stratford-upon-Avon

Goughe, Robert, 118

Gower, John, 148, 200

Grace Church Street. *See* London

Grammar schools. *See* Stratford-upon-Avon

Granville-Barker, Harley, 211

Great Cryptogram. See Donnelly, Ignatius

Greece, 204; literature, 199–202; tragedians, 198; writers, 199

Green Pastures. See Connelly, Marc

Greene, J., 56

Greene, Robert, 35, 71, 93, 120, 201, 202; *Greenes Groatsworth of Wit bought with a million of Repentance*, 94–97, 110, 224

Greene, Thomas, Stratford Town Clerk, 45, 48, 52, 53, 54, 55, 56; diary of, 54–56

Greenwich, 39, 82, 112

Greg, W. W., 180; *A Bibliography of the English Printed Drama to the Restoration*, 227

Grey, Lady Catherine, 17

Griffin, Bartholomew, 156

Groats-worth of Wit. See Greene, Robert

Groundlings, 115

Guild Chapel. *See* Stratford-upon-Avon

Guildhall. *See* London

Gullio, character of, 147, 148

H., Mr. W., 153–54

Hall, Elizabeth, Shakespeare's granddaughter, legacy to, 58

Hall, John, physician, Shakespeare's son-in-law, 32, 43, 46–47, 54, 55, 61, 64, 66; death of, 68; grave of, 68; legacy to, 60, 63

Hall, John, of Worcestershire, 46

Hall, Susanna. *See* Shakespeare, Susanna

Hall's Croft. *See* Stratford-upon-Avon

Halliday, F. E., *Shakespeare, a Pictorial Biography*, 226

Halliwell-Phillipps, J. O., *A Life of William Shakespeare* (1848), 222; *Outlines of the Life of Shakespeare* (1890), 219, 221, 222

Hamlet, character of, 89, 128, 135, 136

Hamlet. See Shakespeare, William

Hampton Court, 82

Hanmer, Sir Thomas, 138, 141

Hannay, Patrick, *A Happy Husband*, 222

Harding (Hardyng), John, the chronicler, 200

Harleian collection, British Museum, 191; Harleian MS 5353, 225; Harleian MS 7368, 227

Harley, Robert. *See* Oxford, Earl of

Harry, 39

Harte, [blank], legacy to, 58

Harte, Joan. *See* Shakespeare, Joan

Harte, Michael, legacy to, 58

Harte, William, legacy to, 58

Harvey, Gabriel, 147, 226

Hastings, Lord, character of, 171

Hathaway, Anne. *See* Shakespeare, Anne Hathaway

Hathaway, Richard, 202

Hay, James. *See* Doncaster

Headboroughs, 91, 111

Hearne, Thomas, 14

Helen of Troy, character of, 156

Helena, character of, 126

Heminges, John, 83–86, 89, 92, 101, 102, 103, 107, 111, 112, 113, 114, 116, 118, 167, 184–90, 192, 193, 194, 195, 203; legacy to, 59, 62

Henley Street. *See* Stratford-upon-Avon

Henrietta Maria, Queen of England, 36

Henry IV, character of, 176

Henry IV, Part 1 and *Part 2*. *See* Shakespeare, William

Henry V, character of, 178

Henry V. See Shakespeare, William

Henry VI, character of, 174

Henry VI, Part 1, Part 2, and *Part 3. See* Shakespeare, William

Henry VII, 40

Henry VIII, 43

Henry VIII. See Shakespeare, William

Henry, Prince of Wales. *See* Prince Henry

Henslowe, Philip, 98; diary of, 229

Herbert, family of, 184–85

Herbert, George, 2

Herbert, Sir Henry, 185

Herbert, Mary. *See* Pembroke, Countess of

Herbert, Philip. *See* Montgomery

Hermione, character of, 65

Hero, character of, 127

Herrick, Robert, 158

Hertford, Edward Seymour, Earl of, 17

Hesiod, 200

Heywood, Thomas, 120, 122, 167–68, 170, 202; *Fair Maid of the Exchange*, 125; *Four Prentices of London*, 169; *Golden Age*, 169; *The Rape of Lucrece*, 227; *Troia Britanica*, 156

Hickson, Samuel, 194

Highway improvement bill, 48–49

Hired men, 89–90, 93, 114

History of Shakespearian Criticism. See Ralli, Augustus

History plays, 123, 126

Hobbes, Thomas, 20

Holland, 151

Holland, Hugh, 188

plague in, see Plague; Public Record Office, see main entry; St. Andrew Undershaft Church, 65; St. Giles, Cripplegate, parish registers, 81, 223; St. Helen's, Bishopsgate, 71, 72, 73; St. Marye Overyes, see St. Saviour's; St. Olave's Church, 80; St. Paul's Cathedral, 76, 115, 163; St. Saviour's Church, Southwark, 80 (burial registers of, 81, fee book, 81, 224); St. Saviour's parish, 105, 106; Somerset House, 57, 113, 114, 222, 225; Southwark, 65, 71, 73, 74; Stationers' Company, see main entry; The Wardrobe, 59

London Prodigal, 177, 195

Longaville, character of, 155

Looney, J. Thomas, *"Shakespeare" Identified in Edward de Vere the Seventeenth Earl of Oxford,* 21

Lord Admiral–Prince Henry's company, 168

Lord Admiral's company, 91, 98

Lord Chamberlain, 162, 185, 186

Lord Chamberlain–King's company, 88–118, 122, 168, 184–86, 189

Lord Chamberlain's company, 11, 71, 75, 91, 98, 99, 100, 101–02, 106, 107, 109, 111, 114, 175, 178, 179, 180; becomes King's company, 111; sharers of, 104. *See also* King's company

Lord Mayor. *See* London

"Lover's Complaint," 157

Love's Labour's Lost. See Shakespeare, William

Love's Labour's Won. See Shakespeare, William

Loves Martyr. See Chester, Robert

Lowin, John, 112, 118

Lucan, 200

Lucas, T., 55

Lucinda, character of, 193

Lucretius, 200

Lucy, Sir Thomas, ballad on, 34

Lute, as legacy, 115

Lydgate, John, 200

Lyly, John, 120, 202, 204

"M., I.," 188

Mabbe, James, 188

Macbeth. See Shakespeare, William

Macbeth, Lady, character of, 126

Macduff, Lady, character of, 128

Macready, William, 211

Magicians, 2

Mainwaring, Arthur, 51, 52, 55, 56

Mainwaring, Humphrey, 43

Malone, Edmond, 74, 76; *An Inquiry into the Authenticity of Certain Miscellaneous Papers and Legal Instruments,* 223

Malone Society Collections, 2, Pt. III (1931), 225, 226

Man, Thomas, 163

Manners, Francis. *See* Rutland, Francis Manners

Manningham, John, diary of, 107–08

Marcellus, character of, 10

Mariana, character of, 183

Marlowe, Christopher, 3, 17, 23, 94, 96, 97, 120, 155, 200, 202, 204; reputation of, 96

Marriage: banns, 29–31; bonds,

Rowe, Nicholas, editor of Shakespeare's plays, 4, 11, 28, 34, 50, 138, 139, 141, 142; *The Works of Mr. William Shakespeare*, 219, 220, 222

Rowington, Manor of, 58

Rowley, William, 120

Rowley of Pembroke Hall, Cambridge, 202

Roydon, Mathew, 201

Russell, Thomas, overseer of will, 60, 61; legacy to, 59

Rutland, Duke of, 224

Rutland, Francis Manners, Earl of, 16, 17, 19; "impresso" for, 82; MS account book, Belvoir Castle, 224

Rutland, Mary Sidney Manners, Countess of, 17

Ryan, Richard, *Dramatic Table Talk*, 219

Sackerson, the bear, 181

Sadler, Hamnet, baker, godfather of Shakespeare's twins, 33, 63; legacy to, 59; witness to will, 61

Sadler, John, 48

Sadler, Judith, godmother of Shakespeare's twins, 33

Saggitary, 140

Sailors, 3

St. Albans, Viscount. *See* Bacon, Sir Francis

St. Andrew Undershaft. *See* London

St. George, patron saint of England, 26

St. Giles, Cripplegate. *See* London

St. Helen's, Bishopsgate. *See* London

St. Marye Overyes. *See* London

St. Olave's. *See* London

St. Paul's. *See* London

St. Saviour's, Southwark. *See* London

Salisbury, Robert Cecil, Earl of, 16, 111

Salisbury Court Theatre, 130

Salisbury's Piece, 54

Sandells, Fulke, 30

Sandfield. *See* Stratford-upon-Avon

Sands, James, apprentice, legacy to, 115

Savage, Thomas, 103

Savoyard Ambassador, 193

Scene division, 138–44

Scene location, 138–44

Scenery, 8, 9

Scenes, 133

Schoolmasters, 27, 35

Scientists, popular estimate of, 2

Scotland, 113

Second Part of the Returne from Parnassus, 108–11

Sejanus His Fall. See Jonson, Ben

Sellengers Round, dance, 110

Seneca, 28, 201, 202

Sermon notes, 107

Settle, Elkanah, and Henry Purcell, *The Fairy Queen*, opera, 207

Sextons, 67

Seymour, Edward. *See* Hertford

Shadwell, Thomas, 194, 207

Shakeshafte, William, actor, 35

Shakespeare, Anne Hathaway, 30–32, 63, 66, 209; cottage of, 32; grave of, 32, 67–68; legacy to, 60, 63; marriage settlement of, 63; second-best bed as legacy to, 62

Shakespeare, Edmund, actor, 80–81

56, 64, 67–68, 220, 221, 222, 223, sexton of, 67); mayor of, 24, 37; municipal records of, 28; New Place. *See main entry;* Old Town Street, 47; Sandfield, 53; schoolmaster's house, 27; Slow Hill Field, 53; taxes, 37; tithes, 43. *See also* Old Stratford

Streat, Peter, 104

Strode, William, 158

Studioso, character of, 109

Sturley, Abraham, 37, 39

Stythe, Thomas, 72

Suffolk, Duke of, character of, 173

Suit, black taffeta, as legacy, 115

Surrey, 73, 75, 76, 92, 105; sheriff of, 74

Sussex, 73

Sussex's company, 173

Swan Theatre, 75, 102, 130; Francis Langley, builder and owner, 75

Swift, Jonathan, 20

Sword, as legacy, 59, 62, 115

Taming of a Shrew, 174, 183, 189–90

Taming of the Shrew. See Shakespeare, William

Tasso, 201

Tate, Nahum, 207

Taverns, 56, 85

Tax collectors, reports of, 71–73

Taxes. *See* Stratford

Taylor, Joseph, 118

Tempest. See Shakespeare, William

Temple Grafton, 31

Terence, 27, 202

Theater: attitude toward, 3; anecdotes, 7–9; managers, 13

Theaters, 34; closed by plague, 147; closing of the, 98; private, 102, 115, 130, 204; proscenium-arch, 132–34; public, 9, 102, 115, 204, 206 (audience at, 130–31, character of, 130–44); shares in, 116. *See also* Bel Savage Inn; Blackfriars Theatre; Bull Inn; Cockpit or Phoenix Theatre in Drury Lane; Cross Keys Inn; Drury Lane Theatre; Fortune Theatre; Globe Theatre; Red Bull Theatre; Salisbury Court Theatre; Swan Theatre; Theatre, The

Theatre, The, 71, 103, 105, 106, 115, 130; destruction of, 104–05

Theobald, Lewis, 138, 139, 193; *Double Falsehood,* 193

Thespis Atticus, 202

Thomas Lord Cromwell, 195

Thoresbie, William, 86

Thorpe, Thomas, 153, 154, 157

Tilts, 82

Tiltyards, 82

Timon Apolloniates, 202

Timon of Athens. See Shakespeare, William

Tire-makers, 76

Tiring house, 131

Tithes, 38

Tithes of Stratford. *See* Stratford-upon-Avon

Titus Andronicus. See Shakespeare, William

Tom of Bedlam, character of, 181

Tomb-makers, 65

Tooley, Nicholas, 118; legacy to, 114

Town halls, 92

Tragical Legend of Robert

THE YALE PAPERBOUNDS